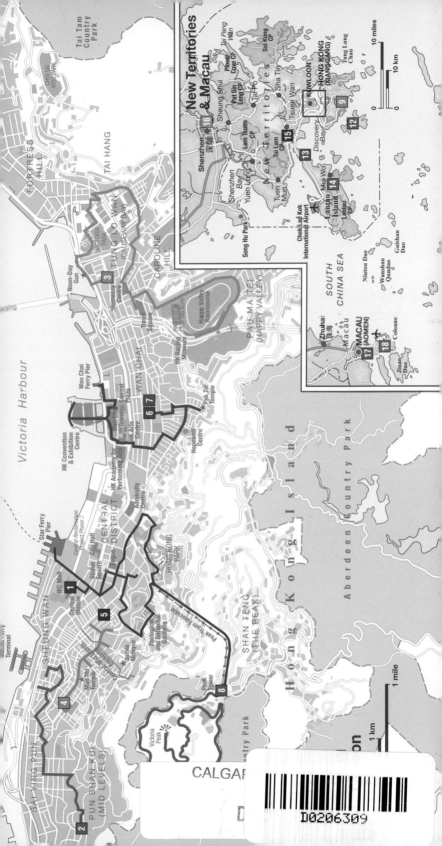

INSIGHT GUIDES

HONG KONG

StepbyStep

APA PUBLICATIONS **L**

Part of the Langenscheidt Publishing Group

CONTENTS

ABOUT THIS BOOK

This *Step by Step Guide* has been produced by the editors of Insight Guides, whose books have set the standard for visual travel guides since 1970. With top-quality photography and authoritative recommendations, this guidebook brings you the very best of Hong Kong in a series of 18 tailor-made tours.

WALKS AND TOURS

The tours in the book provide something for all tastes, budgets and available time. As well as covering Hong Kong's classic attractions and main urban districts, the tours track some lesser-known sights and rural areas; there are also excursions to Shenzhen and Macau for those who want to head further afield.

We recommend that you read the whole of a tour before setting out. This should help you to familiarise yourself with the route and enable you to plan where to stop for refreshments – options for this are shown in the 'Food and Drink' boxes, recognisable by the knife and fork

Above: the sights of Hong Kong.

sign, on most pages. When considering which tour to do, it's worth noting that pounding the streets can be hard going in the hot Hong Kong summer.

OVERVIEW

The tours are set in context by this introductory section, giving an overview of the city plus background information on food and drink, entertainment and shopping. A succinct history timeline shows the key events that have shaped the city over the centuries.

DIRECTORY

Also supporting the tours is the Directory chapter, comprising a user-friendly, clearly organised A–Z of practical information, our pick of where to stay in Hong Kong, and select restaurant listings; these eateries complement the cafés and restaurants that feature within the walks and tours themselves and are intended to offer a wider choice. Also included here are nightlife listings for evening entertainment.

The Author

Ruth Williams arrived in Hong Kong in 1992 for a short stay while travelling in Asia. Like many visitors to Hong Kong she was so taken with the city's energy and endlessly intriguing contrasts that she stayed and made it home. The chance to live in a small village on a green outlying island yet be within 30 minutes of one of the most vibrant cities in the world was of particular appeal; great food, the tropical climate and her fascination with China and Asia were all added attractions. After working in the travel industry and marketing adventure holidays in the Himalayas, she began writing for travel websites and publications. A former editor of the Asian *Maritime Digest*, she is now a regular contributor to *Global Traveler* magazine and various Hong Kong-based publications. An Insight Guide regular, she was the project editor on *Insight Guide Southern China*.

Margin Tips

Shopping tips, historical facts, handy hints and invaluable information on activities to help visitors make the most of their time in Hong Kong.

Feature Boxes

Notable topics are highlighted in these special boxes.

Key Facts Box

This box gives details of the distance covered on the tour, plus an estimate of how long it should take. It also states where the tour starts and finishes, and gives key travel information such as which days are best to do the tour or handy transport tips.

Footers

Look here for the tour name, a map reference and the main attraction on the double page.

Food and Drink

Recommendations of where to stop for refreshment are given in these boxes. The numbers prior to each restaurant/café name link to references in the main text. Restaurants in the Food and Drink boxes are plotted on the maps.

The $ signs at the end of each entry reflect the approximate cost of a three-course meal for one, with a glass of house wine. These should be seen as a guide only. Price ranges, also quoted on the inside back flap for easy reference, are as follows:

$$$$ HK$500 and above
$$$ HK$300–HK$500
$$ HK$150–HK$300
$ HK$150 and below

Route Map

Detailed cartography shows the tour clearly plotted with numbered dots. For more detailed mapping, see the pull-out map, which is tucked inside the back cover.

ARCHITECTURE

Architectural highlights on tour 1 range from the colonial to the contemporary and include some of Hong Kong's best-known buildings. Tour 15 explores the ancient walled villages of the New Territories, while for an injection of European style, head out to Macau (tours 17 and 18).

RECOMMENDED TOURS FOR...

ART BUFFS

Artistic highlights include the art and antiques galleries in the Hollywood Road area (walk 4), the Arts Centre in Wan Chai (walk 6) and items from Chinese antiquities and calligraphy to contemporary art at the Hong Kong Museum of Art (walk 10).

BEACHES

In need of a break from the crowded city? Some of the area's most beautiful beaches are on Southside (tour 9) and around Lamma (walk 14).

CHILDREN

Animal-lovers should visit the pandas, dolphins and other creatures at Ocean Park (tour 9). Science fans may prefer the Space Museum (walk 10). For a big treat, head out to HK Disneyland (tour 13).

EATING OUT

Hong Kong is a wonderful place for eating out, with an endless array of options in the Lan Kwai Fong area (walk 5), Wan Chai (walk 7), Southside (tour 9) and Tsim Sha Tsui (walk 10).

NIGHT OWLS

You will find places that open late across the city, but good starting points for night-time action include Lan Kwai Fong and SoHo (walk 5), Wan Chai (walk 7) and Tsim Sha Tsui (walk 10).

PARKS AND OPEN SPACES

The city itself has three main parks: Hong Kong Park (walk 1), Victoria Park (walk 3) and Kowloon Park (walk 10). For more expansive vistas head up the Peak (walk 8). Much of the New Territories and the islands of Lantau and Lamma (tours 12, 14 and 15) comprise open countryside.

SHOPPERS

The city is famed for its shopping, with options including traditional Chinese stores in Sheung Wan (tour 2), malls in Causeway Bay and Shenzhen (tours 3 and 16), flea markets in Cat Street (tour 4), electronics stores and tailors along Nathan Road (walk 10) and the jade, fish, bird and flower markets (walk 11) of Kowloon.

SPORTY TYPES

A stay in Hong Kong would not be complete without an evening at the Happy Valley races (walk 3). Water-sports are popular at Repulse Bay and Deep Water Bay (tour 9).

TEMPLES AND MONASTERIES

Of the many fine temples in Hong Kong, among the best examples are the Man Mo (walk 4) and Pak Tai Temple (walk 6). The massive bronze Buddha draws the crowds to the Po Lin Monastery (tour 12).

OVERVIEW

An introduction to Hong Kong's geography, customs and culture, plus illuminating background information on food and drink, shopping, entertainment and history.

INTRODUCTION

Hong Kong is one of the most exciting cities in the world, and it is also one of the most straightforward and safe to explore. Signposts are in English as well as Chinese, while inexpensive public transport and taxis make it easy to get around – a welcome bargain in what can be an expensive city.

Covering 1,103 sq km (426 sq miles) Hong Kong, a Special Administrative Region (SAR) of China, can be divided into three parts: Hong Kong Island, the Kowloon peninsula, and the New Territories – which includes the numerous outlying islands.

HONG KONG ISLAND

Hong Kong Island, where the earliest British settlements were established, is now dominated by futuristic buildings housing big banks and lavish hotels. Glamorous shops and restaurants are the norm here, and life moves at a breathless pace. However, among the modernity and awe-inspiring modern architecture this is also the place to find some of Hong Kong's rare colonial buildings and the oldest street market in the city.

A highlight of Hong Kong Island is the Peak, home to a number of magnificent old residences. Gazing down from these rarefied heights reveals just how crowded the city below really is. Pollution and weather permitting, take in the contrasts of skyscrapers, hills and islands and the tiny size of Hong Kong Island at this southern tip of China and all that it has achieved in the last 160 years.

KOWLOON

Set across the harbour from Hong Kong Island (accessible by Mass Transit Railway, Star Ferry or via one of three tunnels), Kowloon offers a taste of the real Hong Kong, with millions of people packed into just a few square kilometres. Nathan Road is the spine of Kowloon, reaching from the impeccable Peninsula Hotel on the Tsim Sha Tsui waterfront towards the Kowloon Hills, which are said to represent nine dragons *(gau lung)* and gave Kowloon its Anglicised name. In between are some of the most densely populated blocks on earth.

Tsim Sha Tsui, Kowloon's southern tip, is the traditional tourist centre of Hong Kong and the site of numerous hotels, bars and shops. It is changing as fast as anywhere in the SAR, with huge developments above and below ground.

At night there's an exciting edge to Kowloon, and while it is often referred to as gritty, it has been certainly been upping the glitz factor in recent years with new skyscrapers, malls and restaurants and plans for a cruise terminal. It also has the city's best museums, lively outdoor markets and bargain clothing, and from Kowloon you can hop on a train to the mainland border or on a through train to Beijing and Shanghai.

Above: swish Sogo shopping mall; Kowloon neon; maid on her day off.

Home Help
While Hong Kong's median income has remained static at HK$10,000 for a decade, many households bring in two incomes or more and rely on live-in foreign domestic helpers to take care of the home, children and elderly relatives.

NEW TERRITORIES AND OUTLYING ISLANDS

Beyond the mountains that ring Kowloon lie the New Territories (NT). A heady mix of empty hillsides, bucolic landscapes and bustling developments, they show a very different side of Hong Kong. Once defined as the land beyond Boundary Street in Kowloon and the Shenzhen River as leased by the British for 99 years in 1898, they are today considered to be the land between the Kowloon Hills and the Chinese border and include the outlying islands.

The New Territories are home to half of Hong Kong's population, most of whom live in purpose-built high-rise new towns such as Sha Tin, although there is also some traditional village housing. Much of the New Territories is made up of unpopulated grassy hills – almost half is designated as country park with mountains, rugged coastlines, beaches and well-marked hiking trails.

A further step into the outfield is offered by the 230-plus outlying islands, which are peaceful rural backwaters. Even Lantau, home to the international airport and a Walt Disney theme park, is largely undeveloped and green.

BEYOND HONG KONG

Macau

To the west across the silt-laden waters of the Pearl River mouth is the former, once sleepy, Portuguese enclave of Macau, now busily reinventing itself as East Asia's leisure capital.

Shenzhen

Across the border with China proper, the city of Shenzhen is well on its way to becoming one of the great financial powerhouses of Asia. It makes a good day trip from Hong Kong for shopping and a taste of the People's Republic.

PEOPLE

Now home to just over 7 million people, Hong Kong's population in its early years as a British colony was closer to 7,000. Since 1850 Hong Kong has absorbed refugees, adventurers and entrepreneurs from all over the world. It has always been predominantly Chinese; today 95 percent

Above from far left: at the opera; at the bird market in Kowloon; Lantau fishermen; the city from above, at night.

Below: outside Tin Hau Temple, Causeway Bay.

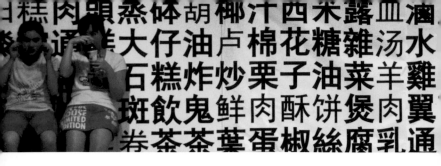

Multilingual

Cantonese is spoken as a first language by most Hong Kong people, and just under half the population declares it can speak English. Increasing numbers are learning Putonghua (Mandarin) for business on the mainland and to communicate with the growing numbers of Putonghua-speaking visitors.

Below: the city streets are crowded with pedestrians.

of the populace is Chinese, almost half were Hong-Kong born, and most call themselves Cantonese. There are over 200,000 foreign domestic helpers, mainly women from the Philippines and Indonesia. In the 2006 census, just over 36,000 respondents described themselves as Caucasian, while almost 85,000 residents are from elsewhere in Asia.

CONFUCIANISM AND CAPITALISM

The Hong Kong Chinese retain traditional Confucian ideals and a strong work ethic. Ancient customs are still observed, and not just by the older generations. Buddhist and Taoist deities are actively worshipped in over 350 temples, and the various religious festivals through the year continue to outstrip their secular cousins in popularity.

Though cynics like to remark that the only culture in Hong Kong is capitalism, and there is no denying that the con-spicuous consumption and ostentatious displays of wealth were abundantly evident from the late 1980s to the mid-1990s, the difficult years that followed this boom period served to correct a very high cost of living and have injected a somewhat humbler philosophy into most walks of life, reflecting a more Confucian perspective.

New Nostalgia

Collective nostalgia, or civic pride, seems to have finally planted itself within the city's consciousness, albeit too late to save some of the best examples of grand colonial-era architecture. Recent plans to level a few of the remaining privately and publicly owned structures have been met with loud opposition.

A recent high-profile example was that of the original Star Ferry Pier in Central – a mere 50 years old, and architecturally undistinguished, but apparently much loved. The government line was that it wasn't old enough to merit preservation (it relocated to a new faux-Edwardian structure).

Likewise, despite public protestations, Queen's Pier, a decades-old standard public jetty in Central, was moved to make way for a new highway and five storey 'groundscraper'. Heritage conservation and debates about what Hong Kong should preserve are now front-page news.

New Confidence

The Hong Kong public, previously preoccupied with securing a foreign passport, should the SAR fall apart, now

has its confidence back and wants to work hard and live well in the city. Meanwhile, the government's current tag line for Hong Kong – Asia's World City – may read a little clumsily, but it takes its cue from the official description from Beijing of the SAR as 'one country two systems'. There is always space for both Confucian values and capitalism in this city.

HANDOVER AND BEYOND

'What has really changed since the handover?' is the perennial question from visitors to residents. Although understandable, it is, however, actually rather irritating, since in reality little has changed because of 1997.

Normal life resumed immediately after Hong Kong's last British governor, Chris Patten, sailed off on the royal yacht in the early hours of 1 July 1997. There were, of course, symbolic changes: the new Hong Kong Special Administrative Region flag fluttered alongside the national flag of China; the word 'Royal' was quickly removed from the institutions that bore it (except, inexplicably, from the Royal Hong Kong Yacht Club, which does fly the SAR flag); and, after the old royal crests were removed, red postboxes were painted green. Streets and buildings named after ex-colonial governors and British royalty and politicians retained their original titles.

Public Protests

The Hong Kong general public, though generally not highly politically motivated, takes to the street regularly when unhappy about social issues. A national holiday in celebration of the establishment of the territory as a SAR, 1 July is one of a few days of the year that demonstrators can be relied upon to air their grievances, which currently include the absence of democratic government elections (politicians are elected from within the Hong Kong Government, rather than by the public) and a lack of a legally endorsed minimum wage.

21st Century

Despite these political issues, Hong Kong today is undeniably confident and optimistic. Having weathered the difficult years from 1998 to 2003, when the Asian economic crisis and two major health scares hit it hard, times are good once again. The one drag for residents is worsening air pollution, partially generated from within, but much also drifting across from industrial plants that line the SAR border in Guangdong, many of which are owned by Hong Kong companies.

For the family tourist Hong Kong Disneyland opened in 2005, and marine-life-themed Ocean Park upped its game, with new rides and attractions on the way and record visitor numbers – in 2007 Beijing presented it with two new pandas in celebration of the 10th anniversary of the handover. There was a host of Hong Kong Government and private sector celebrations in 2007, with most Hong Kong residents relatively satisfied with the life in the SAR a decade on.

Above from far left: Cantonese youth; taxis are cheap and plentiful (except when it's raining).

Climate and When to Go
Hong Kong has a humid subtropical climate, with mild winters, a warm humid spring and a stiflingly hot summer. Best time for exploring on foot is the last three months of the year, when the humidity drops, daytime temperatures average 24°C (75°F) and rain is rare. Winters can be chilly, but temperatures below 10°C (50°F) are unusual. The mercury starts rising in March, April and May, and Hong Kong tends to experience the most rain in late spring and early summer. Typhoon season is June to October (direct hits are rare). Layers and an umbrella are the key to Hong Kong dressing. For more details, see www.weather.gov.hk.

FOOD AND DRINK

Hong Kong has thousands of places in every price range in which to eat and drink, representing almost every national and regional cuisine imaginable. Home-grown highlights include Cantonese food and dim sum.

Below: lunchtime in the city.

Hong Kong people are passionate about eating the best possible food, whether that be a simple noodle dish or an indulgent hotel buffet. Whatever the meal, the locals always have an opinion about the best places to dine. Even the most humble eatery, if good, will gain renown. More cautious eaters should be able to find many of their favourite dishes on offer in Hong Kong, but for those who want to explore new flavours, the city will not disappoint, with its impressive range of restaurants from inexpensive to fine-dining. Adventurous and enthusiastic eaters should have a field day here.

Top-End Dining

On the upscale side, there have never been so many restaurants that deliver truly gourmet dining, often in stylish surroundings with striking harbour views. Lung King Heen (Cantonese) at The Four Seasons and Angelini at the Kowloon Shangri-La are two virtually faultless examples. In the past few years, celebrity chefs have either opened a branch of their restaurants here – the French super-chef Alain Ducasse was the first to do so with Spoon; then came Nobu – or a one-off restaurant in which they are consultant chef, as is the case with Joël Robuchon's Atelier and Pierre Gagnaire's Pierre restaurants. Classic European fine dining in the formal sense remains in established restaurants such as Petrus at the Island Shangri-La and Gaddi's at The Peninsula (both French) and The Verandah (Continental) in Repulse Bay.

CANTONESE FOOD

The Cantonese take huge pleasure in every aspect of eating and joke that they will eat almost anything. People greet one another saying '*Sik Fan?*'

which means 'Eaten rice yet?', placing food at the heart of the culture.

At its best, Cantonese cooking is quick and light, usually stir-fried or steamed to preserve delicate flavours rather than adding heavy amounts of spice. Ginger, spring onions, garlic, soy sauce and rice wine are key ingredients, but Cantonese chefs also use strong flavours such as preserved shrimps, oyster sauce and hoisin sauce for taste.

Chicken and pork are the staple meats of Cantonese fare, while duck, goose, pigeon, fish and seafood are the highlights of a Cantonese banquet. No meal is complete without rice, either steamed or fried, or noodles.

Other Chinese Cuisine

As well as Cantonese food you can find restaurants cooking up almost every type of Chinese cuisine in Hong Kong. From spicy Sichuan prawns and Ma Po Tofu (spicy tofu) to Mongolian hotpots and Peking duck, you can learn a lot about the diversity of China as you eat your way around the city.

INDIAN FOOD

The Indian community has played an important role in Hong Kong, and there are many well-established Indian restaurants in the city. On Hong Kong Island there are lots of good Indian restaurants around Lan Kwai Fong, SoHo and Wan Chai. In Tsim Sha Tsui, overcrowded Chungking Mansions has a host of small, very basic restaurants, often called 'mess clubs', specialising in inexpensive Indian, Pakistani, Afghani and Nepali food.

Above from far left: noodles; Strawberry Tree fruit; blackboard menu; classic Cantonese chicken.

Vegetarian Food
If you are vegetarian, say 'Ngoh seg choi', and then ask for bean-curd (tofu) and veggie options. Seek out Buddhist restaurants for tasty Chinese-style vegetarian food, albeit with somewhat worryingly carnivorous-sounding names.

Below: dim sum.

Smoking

Some dining establishments have a terrace where smoking is permitted, and some still allow it indoors; however, there are fewer of the latter these days, as strict new non-smoking laws, effective from January 2007, are phasing smokers out.

MACAU

The overwhelming number of visitors to Macau may be lured by the prospect of winning at the casinos, but for the culinary adventurer a trip to Macau offers the chance to try the world's first successful fusion cuisine. Macanese food tells the former Portuguese enclave's story well: it is mainly Chinese, with elements of African and Indian spices and hearty Portuguese dishes.

OUT OF TOWN

The New Territories and outlying islands offer laid-back outdoor dining, often with a seafood speciality, as well as roast pigeon. When the weather is fine it is well worth stepping out of the city. Visit Sok Kwu Wan or Yung Shue wan on Lamma Island *(see p.76)* for traditional alfresco dining. And if you are seeking a more international menu, Sai Kung Town, in the New Territories, has friendly restaurants such as Jaspas and Pepporonis, while on Lantau, beautiful Cheung Sha beach has South African-style food at The Stoep *(see p.73)*.

FOOD SHOPPING

Hong Kong people like seeing their food fresh and their chicken and fish

Dim Sum

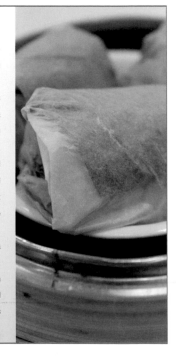

Dim sum is a Hong Kong institution: a kind of Cantonese tapas, traditionally served between breakfast time and lunchtime. Most common are steamed dumplings and savoury buns, rice noodles and pastries. There are scores of varieties. Some restaurants – such as Maxim's Palace in City Hall, Central – still push dishes around in trolleys; ask one to stop and take a look at what's being offered, then order if you like the look of it. Most places, though, now order from dim sum menus, many with pictures. When you are seated, order a pot of tea and your waiter will bring you bowls, chopsticks and a card that is ticked off every time you order another bamboo basket of goodies. The most popular items appear on every dim sum menu: Ha Gao are delicate steamed shrimp dumplings; Siu Mai are a colourful mix of shrimp, minced pork and mushroom inside yellow wonton wrappers; Cha Siu Bao are big, fist-sized fluffy white buns filled with barbecue pork; Ngau Yuk are steamed meatballs made from beef; and Cheung Fan are rolls of white noodle filled with meat or shrimp. You will also find deep-fried spring rolls and wonton and local favourites like chicken's feet and sticky rice wrapped in lotus leaves.

live before they buy if possible, and traditional 'wet markets' supplement the big supermarkets' offerings. To see an old-style food market head to Cross Street in Wan Chai, or step off the Mid-Levels Escalator at Lyndhurst Terrace and walk down Gage Street to Graham Street. This market was established 160 years ago shortly after the colony of Hong Kong was founded. Hawker stalls and open-fronted shops sell an abundance of colourful fruit and vegetables, and the fish is so fresh it's flapping. The stalls and the shops behind them sell everything from household supplies to thousand-year-old eggs, while Chinese medicine shops – crammed full of intriguing mystery items – add to the atmosphere. There are plans afoot to redevelop this area into a brand-new 'Old Shop Street', so this authentic experience of Hong Kong's street life may well disappear.

Most 'wet markets' are now housed in functional, windowless, tiled multi-storey buildings such as Sai Ying Pun market *(see walk 2, p.33–4)*. While not as visually appealing as old-style street markets, they provide an insight into everyday Hong Kong food culture.

FASHIONABLE DINING AND WINING

Trendy establishments in Lan Kwai Fong and SoHo – adjoining neighbourhoods in Central – serve medium- to high-priced fare as the diner is paying for the buzzing atmosphere as much as the food. Many of these places double as bars. Wan Chai has under-gone partial gentrification with a number of similar-style restaurant/bars.

The Kowloon equivalent is found in Knutsford Terrace and Knutsford Steps, in Tsim Sha Tsui, where there are lots of outdoor tables, spilling out from air-conditioned interiors. Nearby in Tsim Sha Tsui East there has been a mushrooming of new restaurants, many with harbour views from their terraces. Happy hours abound, with average operating hours being 5–9pm; ladies' nights allow women to either drink for free or at very reduced prices, most commonly (but not always) on a Wednesday evening. Check local publications' entertainment sections for a fuller picture.

Eating on the Clock
Lunch break for many Hong Kong office workers is strictly between 1pm and 2pm, and this is by far the busiest time on the streets and in the restaurants of the business districts. Be prepared for queues, or simply avoid trying to find a table at 1pm. Go just 30 minutes earlier or later, and you'll find it much easier to get a table.

Below: snake soup is a popular winter dish.

SHOPPING

Hong Kong is often called a shopper's paradise, and it is certainly true that many Hong Kong citizens are insatiable shoppers. Expect to meet temptation everywhere from glitzy malls to bric-a-brac-packed alleys. The main challenge is not to blow the budget.

Above: chops on Chop Alley; children's toys; flowers at a market in Kowloon.

Haggling

As a rule of thumb, most shops don't haggle, but stalls may lower their price a little and give discounts for multiple purchases. If the vendor speaks English, 'Is that your best price?' is a good question to test the water.

In Hong Kong, with land at a premium, cathedral-like shopping malls rather than streets or avenues of stores are the location of posh shops and designer brands. These mega-malls are balanced out by Hong Kong's street markets, which are lively places to shop for inexpensive clothes, gifts and souvenirs and to savour the sights, sounds and smells of life at street level.

MARKETS

In Central visit The Lanes (10am–7pm), which run between Queen's Road and Des Voeux Road Central. Officially known as Li Yuen Street East and Li Yuen Street West, these two narrow lanes are doublelined with shops and stalls selling Chinese-style clothing, cheap clothes, shoes, handbags, watches and souvenirs. Between Hollywood Road and Queen's Road the stone steps of Pottinger Street are lined with stalls selling clothes, hair accessories, haberdashery, shoes and bargain-price fancy-dress costumes, wigs and hats.

Stanley Market

Stanley Market (11am–6pm) on the south coast of Hong Kong Island may be firmly geared to the tourist market, but within this small covered bazaar you will find lots of great gifts, and Stanley is a pleasant place to spend half a day. Look out especially for silk or nylon factory over-runs, sportswear, linens, paintings and pictures.

Kowloon Markets

On Kowloon side Temple Street Night Market (2–10pm) is always an entertaining evening whether you are shopping or browsing after dark. Stalls sell a mix of cheesy souvenirs and T-shirts, kitsch trinkets, clothes, CDs, leather goods and goods from China. Look out for fortune-tellers and Chinese opera singers at the northern end. There are food options here, too: street life is best enjoyed while trying noodles from a stool at a noodle stall.

Other markets in this area are good fun during the daytime: Jade Market, Flower Market, Goldfish Market and the Ladies' Market are all located just off Nathan Road and close to both Mongkok or Yau Ma Tei MTR stations.

WHAT TO BUY

Art, Antiques and Furniture

Hollywood Road is a good place to start looking for antiques and art galleries. Hollywood Centre at 233 Hollywood Road and nearby Cat Street Galleries

have over a dozen small antiques shops within a single building. For larger items catch a taxi to Horizon Plaza on Ap Lei Chau in the south of Hong Kong. This former industrial block has 28 floors of large warehouse-style stores including specialists in antique, reproduction and designer furniture.

Gadgets and Electronics

Electronic items are not the bargain they once were in Hong Kong, but it is still a good place to see the latest innovations. It really is a case of buyer beware and establishing whether the guarantee covers you when you get back home. Citywide chains Fortress (www.fortress.com.hk) and Broadway (www.ibroadway.com.hk) are safe bets. Keen photographers will find professional stores on Lyndhurst Terrace and Stanley Street in Central. The Wan Chai Computer Centre (130 Hennessy Road) is good for accessories and is always packed with technology-loving shoppers.

MALLS

One of the smallest malls is Central's Prince's Building, which has a good selection of exclusive small independent shops selling antiques, jewellery and gifts for the home. Picture This on the third floor is a standout for fans of vintage posters and old maps. Neighbouring Landmark is far swankier, and names such as Harvey Nichols, Louis Vuitton and Gucci abound. The IFC mall has many fans who flock here for its mix of expensive labels and fashion brands such as Zara and Guess.

In Causeway Bay Times Square also has an excellent crosssection of brands, products and price points. All electronic stores are located on the seventh and eighth floors while fashion and footwear are spread over the third, fourth and fifth floors.

If you are exploring the New Territories, you can squeeze some shopping, dinner or a movie in at the end of the day by visiting the vast Festival Walk mall in Kowloon Tong. Elements is an ultramodern new mall above Kowloon station, stuffed with trendy restaurants and smart shops. Close to Star Ferry in Tsim Sha Tsui, Harbour City has an extensive selection of childrenswear, a huge Toys R'Us toy store as well as a broad mix of fashion and lifestyle stores. Night owls can catch the MTR to Kwun Tong station where shops in the APM mall (slogan: play more sleep less) stay open until midnight and restaurants close at 2am.

Above from far left:
Jade Market, Kowloon; pendants shop; abacus on Cat Street; Chinese gold jewellery.

Customer Service
If you are dissatisfied with the standard of service or products purchased in Hong Kong contact the Consumer Council hotline (tel: 2929 2222) or file a complaint at www.consumer.org.hk.

Chinese-Style Wares

Established around 50 years ago, Chinese Arts & Crafts is a reliable store for good-quality Chinese-style clothing, art, jade jewellery and gifts. It will also help you set a benchmark for prices. Look out for its stores in Pacific Place, 59 Queen's Road Central, the China Resources Building in Wan Chai, and Star House in Tsim Sha Tsui. For a more stylish interpretation of the Chinese aesthetic, visit Shanghai Tang *(right)* in Pedder Street Central, while GOD stores in Causeway Bay or Hollywood Road Central are the place to go for a more youthful witty take.

ENTERTAINMENT

There's always something going on in Hong Kong, regardless of the month you visit, from traditional Chinese festivals to international arts events and fringe theatre productions.

What's On When
The HKTB tourist packs at airports and border crossings contain extensive details on all events in town each month. The *South China Morning Post*, *HK Magazine* and *Time Out Hong Kong* all have daily and weekly updates on what's on. Check www.discover hongkong.com for more information.

ARTS FESTIVALS

Festivals play a large part in Hong Kong's entertainment calendar. The annual Hong Kong Arts Festival (tel: 2824 3555; www.hk.artsfestival.org), running through February and early March, features the best Hong Kong and Chinese artists as well as first-class international performers from Youssou N'Dour to the Royal Shakespeare Company. Performances are mainly held in City Hall, the Hong Kong Cultural Centre and the Academy for Performing Arts. The City Festival is organised from the Fringe Club each January, with three weeks of new and alternative concerts, performances, art exhibits, street events and more.

World-renowned authors come to the city in March for the Man Hong Kong International Literary Festival (www.festival.org.hk). Also in March – and through April – is the Hong Kong International Film Festival (www.hkiff.org.hk). The Le French May (www.lefrenchmay.com) extends throughout the summer and promotes all kinds of arts, with a French connection.

THEATRE

Most local theatre productions are in Cantonese, though some of the larger venues will run English and Mandarin subtitles. Professional theatre groups such as Chung Ying Theatre Company (www.chungying.com) and Zuni Icosohedron (www.zuni.org.hk) present some challenging pieces with and without subtitles, while Hong Kong Reparatory Theatre produces Chinese and international drama, in Cantonese with English subtitles.

DANCE

Hong Kong has a vibrant dance scene and a number of dance companies in permanent residence. Hong Kong Dance Company (www.hkdance.com) draws on Hong Kong's cultural mix and adheres to a belief that dance derives from tradition but is not restricted by boundaries. Committed to maintaining Chinese dance, the acclaimed company performs traditional folk dances and dance dramas as well as original works incorporating Western techniques. City Contemporary Dance Company (www.ccdc.com.hk) is Hong Kong's leading modern dance company, renowned for its distinctive and diverse style of programmes. Hong Kong Ballet (www.hkballet.com) is one of the foremost classical ballet companies in Asia and presents a broad-based repertoire including the classics.

CLASSICAL MUSIC

The Hong Kong Philharmonic Orchestra (HKPO; www.hkpo.com), one of Asia's leading orchestras, presents over 150 performances each year, from core symphonic classics to collaboration with Canto-pop artists. The HKPO Hong Kong Sinfonietta (www.hksinfonietta.org) performs over 70 times a year, mainly at Hong Kong City Hall, and is renowned for its innovative audience development concerts, crossover productions and new commissions.

ROCK AND POP

Scratch under the surface and Hong Kong's live music scene is there to be found. Starting points for investigating the underground music scene are venues such as Rockschool *(see p.123)* and the Fringe Club *(see p.122)*. Underground HK (www.undergroundhk.com) and Shazza Music (www.shazzamusic.com) both promote independent artists.

Canto-pop – a type of saccharine pop music – is hugely popular in Hong Kong. Big names include teen idols Eason Chan, and Twins.

FILM

Hong Kong may not be making as many movies as it once did, but the influence of the home-grown film studios is more widely recognised than ever thanks to the recent Hollywood success of director John Woo, actors Michelle Yeow, Chow Yun-Fat and the irrepressible Jackie Chan.

Oscar wins for Martin Scorsese's remake of Andrew Lau and Alan Mak's Hong Kong crime-thriller *Infernal Affairs* and period kung-fu *Crouching Tiger, Hidden Dragon* (a joint production between Hong Kong, mainland China, Taiwan and the US), plus the appeal of Bruce Lee's movies, all keep the city's movie industry in the spotlight.

For a taste of modern Hong Kong movies, watch films by art-house director Wong Kar Wai *(Chungking Express, In the Mood For Love)* or the outrageous Fruit Chan *(Little Cheung, Made in Hong Kong, Durian Durian)*.

Recent home-grown hits include *Echoes of the Rainbow,* which depicts life in 1950s Hong Kong. Funded by the government's film development fund (designed to revive the local movie industry), the movie had the unexpected side effect of stopping government plans to demolish Wing Lee Street where the film was shot. The Sun Yat-Sen 2009 biopic *Bodyguards and Assassins*, notable for Nicholas Tse's award-winning performance as a rickshaw driver, showcases 21st-century Hong Kong movie-making and the city's revolutionary past.

NIGHTLIFE

Hong Kong Island's nightlife is largely centred around Lan Kwai Fong, Wyndham Steet and SoHo in Central and Wan Chai. In Kowloon, TST and TST East have an increasing number of venues with outdoor seating and harbour views that are popular with visitors and locals alike. See Nightlife *(p.122)* for recommendations.

Above from far left: detail of a dragon boat; lion dances are performed to usher in the Lunar New Year.

Major Festivals
Chinese New Year (CNY), also known as Spring Festival, Is celebrated on the first moon of the first month of the New Year, falling in late January or early to mid February. Businesses shut down for three days in Hong Kong, and a week on the mainland. On New Year's Day night the Hong Kong Tourist Board (HKTB) organises a huge parade with lion dancers, performers and floats; Wong Iai Sing Temple is the place to go for a traditional experience. Other major festivals include the Bun Festival, hosted by the island of Cheung Chau. Highlights include processions, and the construction of a plastic bun tower, outside the Pak Tai Temple. Also notable is the Dragonboat Festival, held around Stanley, Lamma and Lantau in spring and early summer. Crews of 20 or 30 take to the water in 10m- (33ft-) long boats fronted by a dragon's head.

HISTORY: KEY DATES

Initially regarded by the British as an ill-chosen gain of limited value, Hong Kong soon became an important part of the Empire – and one that was only reluctantly relinquished. The city is now thriving as a Special Administrative Region, under the rule of the Chinese Communist Party.

EARLY HISTORY

*c.***4000** BC	Aborigines set up Stone-Age settlements in coastal areas.
AD **1577**	Portugal establishes official trading colony at Macau.
1662	Imperial edict aimed at quelling rebels and pirates forces coastal dwellers to uproot and move inland.
1669	Evacuation edict is reversed and coastal areas repopulated by Hakka people from northern China.
1714	Canton (Guangzhou) opened to foreign trade; the British East India Company (EIC) is established.
1773	The EIC unloads 68kg (150lb) of Bengal opium at Canton.
1799	China bans opium trade but the lucrative drug, used as trading currency, continues to be smuggled.
1839	Commissioner Lin Tse-hu confiscates more than 20,000 chests of opium from British traders, sparking off the First Opium War.
1841	Britain takes unofficial possession of Hong Kong Island.

COLONIAL PERIOD

1842	Hong Kong Island officially ceded to Britain under Treaty of Nanking.
1860	Kowloon Peninsula and Stonecutters Island ceded to Britain as part of the Convention of Peking following the Second Opium War.
1898	Britain negotiates a 99-year lease of the New Territories and Outlying Islands.
1911	Qing dynasty falls; Sun Yat-sen forms the Republic of China.
1938	Canton falls to Japan. Refugees flee to Hong Kong.
1941	Hong Kong falls to invading Japanese on Christmas Day.
1945	World War II ends and Hong Kong is liberated on 30 August.
1949–53	Communist victory on mainland China sees massive waves of refugees swell the local population. Industrialisation commences.
1954	Government initiates public-housing programmes, following the mushrooming of unsanitary squatter settlements.
1966–7	Pro-Communist riots inspired by the Cultural Revolution in China.
1973	First of several New Towns opened in Tuen Mun, New Territories.

Colonial Approach
'Albert is so amused,' wrote Queen Victoria, 'at my having got the island of Hong Kong.' Her foreign secretary, Lord Palmerston, was not so amused; he famously dismissed Hong Kong as 'a barren island with hardly a house upon it.'

1975	The first Vietnamese boat people arrive, sparking over two decades of refugee camps; thousands are repatriated before the 1997 handover.
1979	Mass Transit Railway opens.
1984	Margaret Thatcher and Chinese premier Zhao Ziyang sign a declaration that Hong Kong will revert to Chinese rule in 1997.
1992	Governor Chris Patten appointed the last British colonial head.
1995	A fully elected Legislative Council (LegCo) is voted into power as part of Patten's push for more democracy.

Above from far left: the British negotiate to open Chinese ports; the Japanese invade in December 1941.

HANDOVER AND BEYOND

1997	China resumes sovereignty, Tung Chee-hwa appointed Chief Executive of the newly named Hong Kong Special Administrative Region (SAR), as LegCo is briefly replaced by Provisional Legislature.
1998	Elections held for LegCo. New airport opens at Chek Lap Kok. The Hong Kong Stock Market dives on the back of the Asian economic crisis. Avian flu threatens outbreaks from this year.
1999	Rule of law is undermined, as government asks Beijing to overturn Court of Final Appeal's ruling on the right of abode.
2000	Elections for second four-year term of office for LegCo.
2002	Tung Chee-hwa made Chief Executive for second five-year term.
2003	Hong Kong struggles with a weak economy; 299 people killed by the Sars virus. On 1 July over 500,000 people march against Article 23, a controversial anti-subversion bill.
2004	Beijing rules out universal suffrage by 2007.
2005	Civil servant Donald Tsang made second HKSAR Chief Executive.
2006	China booms and Hong Kong economy surges. 25.25 million people visit Hong Kong; 13 million are tourists from the mainland.
2007	Donald Tsang re-elected. HKSAR celebrates 10th anniversary.
2008	Hong Kong hosts equestrian events for the Beijing 2008 Olympics.
2009	Consumer and business confidence returns to pre-recession levels.
2010	Five LegCo members resign to pressure Beijing for full democracy.

Above: relief decoration, Po Lin Monastery.

Below: the famous skyline of Hong Kong Island viewed from Kowloon.

WALKS AND TOURS

CENTRAL DISTRICT

After breakfast at an IFC or Exchange Square café, explore Central and its awe-inspiring new architecture, St John's Cathedral and the Zoological and Botanical Gardens. Take the Peak Tram up to the Peak and stop for lunch, then head back via Hong Kong Park, Flagstaff House and another tram ride.

DISTANCE 5km (3 miles)
TIME Half to a full day
START Hong Kong Airport
Express Station, Exit B2
END Central Ferry Piers 7 and 8
GETTING AROUND
This is mainly a walking tour, with
trips on the Peak Tram and a double-
decker city tram to cover longer or
steeper sections and to add variety.

This tour is designed to give you a feel for Central District, the hub of wealth and power in Hong Kong since the British first took possession of this barren rock on the coast of China in 1841. This is ideally a weekday itinerary, to capture the feeling of the business and financial centre in action. On Sundays and public holidays thousands of predominantly Filipina domestic helpers, enjoying their only time off, gather to picnic and socialise

on Central's walkways and squares, which makes for a festive atmosphere; note, however, that many of the buildings in this area are roped off.

EXCHANGE SQUARE

From the Hong Kong terminus of the Airport Express line, take the elevator to Level One and walk through the IFC Mall *(see below)* to **Exchange Square** ❶, home to the Hong Kong Stock Exchange. You can stop for breakfast at one of the many coffeeshops in the IFC, such as **Simplylife**, see ⑪①, or outside The Forum in Exchange Square, for example **La Fontaine**, see ⑪②. If you're early enough, you might see people practising tai chi; otherwise, enjoy the people-watching, and admire the large bronze sculptures: *Tai Chi* by Ju Ming, Henry Moore's *Oval with Points* and the two life-size *Water Buffalo* by Dame Elisabeth Frink.

Two IFC

Looming largest of all above the three towers of Exchange Square and the vast International Finance Centre (IFC) is Hong Kong's second-tallest building, **Two IFC** ❷. Completed in 2003, at 415m (1,362ft) it is currently the sixth-tallest building in the world. Angelina Jolie leaps off the top of it in the movie *Lara Croft Tomb Raider: The Cradle of Power*. IFC includes the Hong Kong MTR and Airport Express Station, the One and Two IFC office towers. IFC Mall has hundreds of shops, a cosy cinema and dozens of cafés and restaurants with wonderful views of the harbour.

CENTRES OF POWER

Now follow the elevated walkway east beyond One Exchange Square and take the second bridge on the right across Connaught Road, then through Chater House. Make your way down to street level, turn left down Chater Road and walk towards the **Mandarin Oriental Hong Kong** ❸ hotel.

First opened in 1963, this impressive hotel is home to Hong Kong institutions such as the Captain's Bar and the Mandarin Grill, where the city's movers and shakers have gathered for decades. Rose-petal jam or handmade chocolates from the Mandarin Cake Shop make great gifts.

Cross the road to **Statue Square** ❹, so-called because it originally housed statues of Queen Victoria, Prince Albert and Edward VII when it was opened in 1902.

Food and Drink 🍴

① SIMPLYLIFE BREAD AND WINE
Podium level 1, IFC Mall; tel: 2234 7356; $–$$
Top coffee plus pastries and sandwiches to take away or eat in. It's hard not to stay though, as the whole of one side is floor-to-ceiling picture windows facing the harbour.

② LA FONTAINE
The Forum, Exchange Square, Central; tel: 2537 2938; $–$$
French-style patisserie La Fontaine has expanded to serve hot lunches, sandwiches and salads to executives working in the financial district. Breakfast sets are good value at under HK$40 from 7.30–11am.

Above from far left: Central District seen from Kowloon at night; the Mid-levels escalator.

Opposite: the Former Supreme Court Building (1912), a rare historic presence in Central, has been home to the Legislative Council since 1985; poster from the more contemporary IFC Mall.
Opposite below: serving tea.

Shortcuts
When the humidity and temperature rise or rainstorms hit, Hong Kongers are experts at crossing town via the pedestrian walkways linking malls and office buildings. In Central and Admiralty you can walk between 40 buildings along 7km (4 miles) of walkways without ever going outside.

Lucky Lions

HSBC's two bronze lions were cast in Shanghai in 1935. Bullet marks from the Battle of Hong Kong (1941) can be traced on the pair, and like all the statues in Statue Square the lions were removed during the Japanese occupation. Fortunately, they did not end up in the smelter and were rediscovered in Japan after the war and returned to Hong Kong.

LegCo and the Club

The Neoclassical **Former Supreme Court Building ❺**, on the east side of Statue Square, was built in 1912. Since 1985 it has been the home of Hong Kong's governing body, the Legislative Council (LegCo), although they are set to move to a new building when the Tamar Government Headquarters are completed in 2011. Alongside the LegCo building are the cenotaph commemorating the dead of World War I and the Chater Gardens. Overlooking all this is the city's exclusive Hong Kong Club, housed in a building of the same name (1980) by the Australian architect Harry Seidler.

The only statue in the square is that of banker Sir Thomas Jackson, one of the foremost early managers of the Hongkong & Shanghai Bank (HSBC), which opened its first headquarters across the road to the south of the square in 1865.

'The Bank'

Cross Des Voeux Road to explore the HSBC **Headquarters Building ❻**. Designed in 1985 by the British architect Norman Foster, it is recognised as one of the world's most innovative struc-

tures, due to its exo-skeleton and lack of internal support. Pass the two bronze lions *(see left)* that guard the front of the building, to walk underneath and gaze up at its 'guts' through the glass floor. During banking hours you can take an escalator up to the main public hall on level 3 for a closer inspection.

Afterwards, continue heading inland, away from the harbour, across the footbridge over Queen's Road Central to Battery Path.

COLONIAL REMINDERS

Once over the bridge, turn left up banyan-shaded Battery Path, past the elegant red-brick Court of Final Appeal Building (closed to visitors), dating from 1917 and also known as the Former French Mission Building, to **St John's Cathedral ❼** (daily 7am–6pm). Dwarfed by the soaring cathedrals of commerce all around it, this fine Victorian Gothic building was consecrated in 1849. Pause just for a moment to take in the peaceful interior, with its turquoise timber ceiling and gently whirring fans. There are views across to the soaring Bank of China building nearby.

From here, either take a footbridge across Garden Road to the Peak Tram terminus or take a detour around some more colonial sites.

Hilly Hong Kong

To continue the tour, return to Queen's Road Central down Battery Path, then take the second left into Duddell Street, climbing the steps at the far end.

Food and Drink 🍴

③ FRINGE CLUB

2 Lower Albert Road, Central; tel: 2521 7251; $–$$

A good place to stop for a refreshing beverage any time from noon to midnight. The Fotogallerie has a vegetarian lunch buffet Mon–Fri noon–2.30pm. Dine inside the gallery or head upstairs to the roof terrace. After lunch, a light tapas-style menu is served into the evening in Fotogallerie and on the roof. The main bar also has exhibitions and live music. *See also p.122.*

The quaint gas lamps at the top and bottom of the steps are more than 100 years old and are the only ones that are still in active service in Hong Kong.

At this point, turn right to follow the curve of Ice House Street, past a cluster of old colonial buildings. Straight ahead is the red-brick **Dairy Farm Building**, which was built as an ice house in the late 19th century and first restored in 1913. It now houses a variety of institutions, from the members-only Foreign Correspondents' Club to Hong Kong's foremost alternative arts venue, the **Fringe Club** ➑, which hosts exhibitions, music, theatre and performances and has a roof garden and restaurant, see ⑪③.

To the left are Bishop's House (1850) and St Paul's Episcopal Church (1911). Lan Kwai Fong and Wyndham Street *(see p.43)*, with their plethora of

(see p.43)

Above from far left: sunset over Central and the Star Ferry; HSBC lion; the Shanghai Tang store sells classy chinoiserie; view of St John's Cathedral.

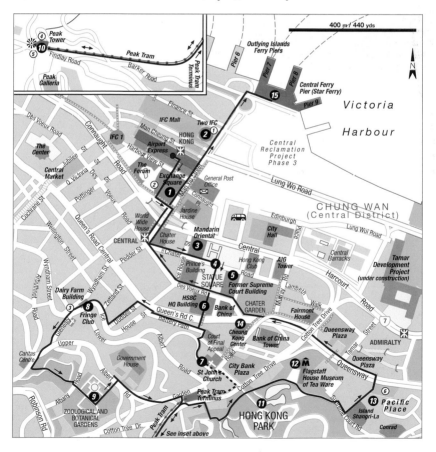

restaurants open from lunchtime onwards, are just around the corner.

The Zoo and Botanical Gardens
Head up Glenealy, veering right at the 'Ped Subway' sign and public toilets, through a subway. Turn left opposite the Caritas Centre into the **Hong Kong Zoological and Botanical Gardens ⑨** (daily 6am–7pm; free). The zoo is tiny and old-fashioned by international standards, but the botanical gardens, established in 1864, offer a pleasant green retreat a short stroll from the middle of the city.

Exit from the gardens' eastern end and negotiate your way across the Upper Albert Road junction by two flights of steps. Take a slight detour left along Upper Albert Road to view the front of Government House (1855), which was the official residence of 25 of Hong Kong's 28 British Governors. Since 2004 it has been the home of the HKSAR's Chief Executive, Donald Tsang.

Now retrace your steps along Upper Albert Road across Garden Road and follow the signs to Hong Kong Park and the Peak Tram station, under the Cotton Tree Drive flyover.

UP TO THE PEAK

In continuous operation since 1888, the 'Peak Tram' is actually a funicular railway, built to serve the wealthy residents of the Peak who previously had to rely on human-carried sedan chairs for transport to the waterfront. Trams depart every 10 to 15 minutes from 7am to midnight for a breathtaking journey to the summit.

Exit at the **Peak Tower ⑩** and head up the escalators to the rooftop **Sky Terrace** (charge). The 360-degree panoramic views from the top are magnificent on a clear day. You can stop for lunch at any of the Peak Tower's 11 restaurants and cafés, see ⑪④, or head outside to Café Deco in the Peak Galleria or the **Peak Lookout**, see ⑪⑤, just across the road. For a longer exploration of the Peak, consult the Victoria Peak walk (see p.54).

Down to Hong Kong Park
Return downhill on the Peak Tram. Exit the station, and turn right under the Cotton Tree Drive flyover into **Hong Kong Park ⑪** (daily 7am–11pm). Wander round the high-tech aviary and greenhouses, see couples posing for photos in full wedding

Above: old Bank of China lion; antique teapot at Flagstaff House; in Hong Kong Park.

Food and Drink 🍴

④ PEARL ON THE PEAK
Level 1, The Peak Tower; tel: 2849 5123; $$$$
Glamorous restaurant with spectacular floor-to-ceiling views. An offshoot of Melbourne's Pearl restaurant, it serves what chef Geoff Lindsay describes as modern Australian cuisine, with creative Asian and Turkish flavours.

⑤ PEAK LOOKOUT
121 Peak Road; tel: 2849 1000; $$
An old-world setting for excellent Asian and European food: everything from tandoori and teriyaki to pasta, barbecue and grills. Dine inside the stone lodge or head outdoors for the lovely garden terrace and views down the hill to Aberdeen.

⑥ PEKING GARDEN
Shop 003, Pacific Place; tel: 2845 8452; $$
Lively restaurant offering northern Chinese food: Peking duck carving exhibitions are a speciality.

regalia by the registry office, or climb the 105 steps of the observatory tower for another sweeping view. Another reason to come here is to visit the **Flagstaff House Museum of Tea Ware** ⑫ (Wed–Mon 10am–5pm; free). Constructed in 1846, the house is the oldest European structure still standing in Hong Kong. It served as the residence of the Commander-in-Chief of the British Forces for more than 130 years, but now hosts intriguing exhibits on everything to do with tea and also has a nice tearoom.

MODERN SPIRES

Leave the park by the Supreme Court Road exit. Take the elevator on your left down to **Pacific Place** ⑬, a vast hotel and shopping complex that also has enjoyable places to eat, such as **Peking Garden**, see ⑪⑥. If you're not in the mood for shopping, follow the signs for Admiralty MTR station and Queensway Plaza, reached via a pedestrian bridge over Queensway. Halfway across, take the steps down to the tramway and ride three stops on a westbound tram.

High Finance

The first stop takes you as far as the **Bank of China** ⑭ (1989), a spectacular prism-like structure designed by Sino-American architect I.M. Pei and, at 70 storeys (367m/1,204ft), the fourth tallest in town. Next door the dull design of the Cheung Kong Centre (1999) has prompted the nickname the 'box the Bank of China came in'. Its 283m/927ft height is said to have been determined

by drawing a line between the Bank of China and HSBC headquarters.

Chater Garden opposite, once home of the exclusive Hong Kong Cricket Club, is now a pleasant urban open space. The tramline wraps around the Art Deco-style old Bank of China Building (1950), and stops outside the HSBC at Statue Square. Squeeze your way to the front of the tram to pay your fare, so you can get off at the next stop.

Get off at World Wide House, then head towards the harbour along Pedder Street via the footbridge across four-lane Connaught Road. Pass Jardine House and the main Post Office to your right and follow the walkway to the waterfront. To your left is IFC; to the right look over newly reclaimed land towards Wan Chai. From here you can see your final destination, the new but Edwardian-style **Central Ferry Pier** ⑮ (2006). Catch a Star Ferry across to Kowloon from piers 7 or 8, and get a full view of the Hong Kong skyline.

The Skyline Competition

Seen from the top of the Peak or the Star Ferry, Hong Kong's rocketing skyline is an awe-inspiring symbol of its energy. One extraordinary thing about it is how recent it is: two prime landmarks, the HSBC and Bank of China, only date from the 1980s, and its biggest tower, Two IFC, was completed in 2004. On the Kowloon side building was long restricted by the proximity of Kai Tak airport, but since the new airport opened in 1998 this area has become a new developers' playground. The tallest building in the city is now the 118-storey International Commerce Centre (ICC), 480m (1,588ft) above Kowloon station and surrounded by a cluster of high-end high-rise residential towers topping 200m (660ft).

WESTERN DISTRICT

Contrasting atmospheres: the calm campus of Hong Kong University and then the tightly packed, oldest Chinese districts of Sai Ying Pun and Sheung Wan, with their constant street life and fascinating shops.

> **DISTANCE** 3km (2 miles)
> **TIME** Half a day
> **START** HK University
> **END** Sheung Wan MTR
> **POINTS TO NOTE**
> The best way to use this walk is as a base for wandering and exploring the alleys and sidestreets of these residential and trading districts. The route is flat apart from the steep walk downhill along Centre Street.

Below: decorative fountain in Western.

This tour concentrates on one of the oldest, least 'modernised' parts of Hong Kong, the atmospheric streets and alleyways of Sai Ying Pun and Sheung Wan, west of Central. Less hectic than Kowloon, this is everyday Hong Kong street life, where open-fronted 'shop-houses' and family businesses, not mega malls and brands, set the tone. Along the main streets, goods from the trading houses and shops overflow onto the pavements with a mix of everything from daily necessities to traditional Chinese medicine, 'hell money' and dim sum baskets.

Start on a more relaxed note, though, at the campus of Hong Kong University (HKU) in Pok Fu Lam. Take a 3A, 7 or 91 bus from the Central Ferry Pier bus terminal and get off on Pok Fu Lam Road when you see the sign for Hong Kong University, and (on your right) the modern Haking Wong Building.

THE UNIVERSITY

Founded at the start of the 20th century, **Hong Kong University** ❶ is now one of Asia's leading academic institutions, with 10,000 students. Enter the campus at the West Gate on Pok Fu Lam Road, with steps leading up to the Haking Wong Building on your right. Turn left to enter the original campus, beneath shady trees.

To the right, the Main Arts Building is a stately Edwardian structure with internal courtyards and graceful palms. The 1910 foundation stone reveals that Indian businessman H.N. Mody, a 'Parsi gentleman, 50 years resident in Hong Kong', funded this first university building. Across the path the graceful Hung Hing Ying Building, constructed in 1919, houses the Music Department (open to the public for recitals).

University Museum and Art Gallery
Follow the driveway round to Bonham Road and the **University Museum and Art Gallery ❷** (tel: 2241 5500; www.hku.hk/hkumag; Mon–Sat 9.30am–6pm, Sun 1.30–5.30pm; free). The 1930s Fung Ping Shan Building contains a diverse collection of early Chinese bronzes, ceramics and other artefacts, including a unique set of bronze crosses made by the Nestorians, a Christian community who have lived in China since around AD 600. There are also fine Ming and early Qing paintings, while contemporary Chinese art is exhibited in the TT Tsui Building alongside, linked by a footbridge. Pause to enjoy some Chinese tea at the museum's **Tea Gallery**, see ⑪①.

SAI YING PUN

Leaving the University, head back eastwards on Bonham Road, and shortly after the grey columns and the brick of King's College school, which was founded in 1926, turn left down pedestrianised **Centre Street ❸**. This area is called Sai Ying Pun: *Sai* means west, *Ying Pun* means military camp, and this was where the first British camps were established in the 1840s.

The section below High Street retains a flavour of an older Hong Kong, with small earth god shrines outside each shop, even though modern indoor markets have replaced outdoor stalls along the steep street. Today locals shop at **Sai**

Above from far left: elderly couple out for a walk; delivery by hand; tea shop; local fashion designer.

Food and Drink

① TEA GALLERY
University Museum and Art Gallery, TT Tsui Building, 94 Bonham Road; $
Tea is served in miniature pots and porcelain cups at four traditional rosewood tables on the gallery's lower floor. Novices are encouraged to brew up themselves: a 'how-to' guide is provided.

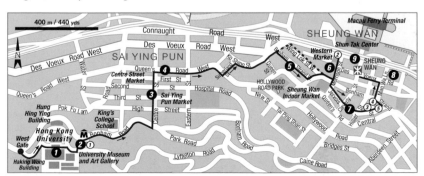

Above from left: statues and historic buildings in Sheung Wan; decorative chops (Chinese seals).

Above: practitioner in Chinese medicine; young shopkeeper on Chop Alley.

Below: 'hell' money.

Ying Pun Market at the junction of Centre and Second for meat, fish and vegetables, while **Centre Street Market** sells cheap clothes and household items.

First Road in Hong Kong

As you walk down Centre Street you cross Third, Second and First streets until you reach **Queen's Road**, the first road built in Hong Kong after the British claimed the island in 1841.

FUNERAL SHOPPING

Turn right at the corner – past a Cantonese-style cooked meat shop – onto **Queen's Road West ❹**, and then walk for a few minutes until you reach a row of shops on the right selling floral wreaths, joss sticks, sacks of 'hell' money, paper offerings and brass urns, which are true boutiques for the deceased: everything you need for a traditional Chinese funeral can be found here except for coffins, which are supplied by coffin shops not far away on Hollywood Road. Keeping up with the times, paper items for the afterlife now include speedboats, planes, microwave ovens, mobile phones and flat-screen televisions.

SHEUNG WAN BAZAAR

Cross Queen's Road West and cut down Sutherland Street and turn right along Ko Shing Street. Browse the shops selling traditional Chinese medicines, dried foods, shrimps, starfish and tubs of exotic-looking items, and take in the pungent aromas.

Continue on Des Voeux Road West to reach, on your right, **Bonham Strand West ❺**, where the shops deal wholesale in items prized in traditional Chinese medicine and cuisine – ginseng, antelope horn, sharks' fin, birds' nests and abalone. This area is also at the centre of the global trade in shark fins.

Western Market

Heading back to Central, cross **Sheung Wan Fong**, a busy little piazza. Elderly citizens rest under palm trees, while shoppers dodge deliveries dispersed by trolleys and bikes. On your right is a 12-storey civic centre that packs in a wet market with leisure facilities.

Head left down On Tai Street, past stalls selling dried food, takeaway noodles, and fruit and vegetables, to reach **Western Market ❻**, built in 1906. Used as a fresh produce market for more than 80 years, this handsome, European-looking red-brick building was restored in 1991 as a period

shopping mall. You'll find interesting memorabilia, handicrafts, toys, jewellery and other gifts on the ground floor, and fabric merchants selling everything from Chinese silk to Harris tweed upstairs. Prices are fair, and the merchants know their stuff; they moved here when the legendary 'Cloth Alley' bazaar on Wing On Street was closed down to make way for high-rise office towers. Upstairs at the **Grand Stage**, see ⑪②, the afternoon tea-dances add to the old-world atmosphere and charm.

The Heart of Sheung Wan

Go back up Morrison Street to explore **Sheung Wan** further. Turn left into **Jervois Street** ❼, which marked the waterfront until the first harbour reclamation began in 1852; signs for ships' chandlers remind you of the area's past.

Cleverly Street has a shady sitting-out area next to a caged bird shop. Local bird fanciers gather here with their prized possessions. At 13 Hillier Street is one of Hong Kong's fabled reptile shops, selling, among other things, snakes for soup, wine, and other traditional recipes popular during winter months.

Shops that have been selling rice, herbs, specialist teas, noodles, preserved fruits and Chinese sweets for 60 to 100 years are interspersed with the more everyday shops selling hardware, fruit and flowers, as well as a posh French delicatessen (Monsieur Chatté, 121 Bonham Strand). There are some good inexpensive cafés and restaurants serving the local office workers around here, see ⑪③, ④ and ⑤.

Chop Alley

At the end of Jervois Street turn left back onto Bonham Strand. Turn right just after a branch of the HSBC bank, into **Man Wa Lane** ❽, also known as 'Chop Alley'. Chop-makers have been plying their trade here since the 1920s, carving traditional Chinese seals or 'chops' from stone, jade, bone or ivory; the art itself is some 3,000 years old. Chop-makers will translate your name and carve a custom chop in one to four hours.

Turn left on Wing Lok Street for **Sheung Wan MTR station** ❾; alternatively, follow the lane to Des Voeux Road and hop on a tram, or wander slowly east along Des Voeux Road, exploring yet more narrow lanes that connect it to Queen's Road.

Local Delicacies

Snakes are considered a wintertime 'delicacy', as the meat and body fluids are believed to fortify the human body against the cold; geckos, on the other hand, are on the menu all year round.

Food and Drink

② THE GRAND STAGE
2/F Western Market, 23 Des Voeux Road, Sheung Wan; tel: 2815 2311; $$
This restaurant on the top floor of Western Market serves familiar dim sum and Cantonese favourites. After 2.30pm, tables are pushed back, and ballroom dancers take to the floor.

③ MALAY MAMA
11A Mercer Street, Sheung Wan; tel: 2542 4111; $
Noodle fans pack into this no-frills Malaysian café that specialises in hearty bowls of Laksa, Ipoh Ho Fun and Prawn Mee.

④ MASALA
10 Mercer Street, Sheung Wan; tel: 2581 9777; $
Friendly Indian restaurant with a wide choice of dishes. Standouts include bhindi masala, fish madras, tarka dhal and tandoori chicken. Excellent-value set menus.

⑤ CAFÉ ROMA
1 Jervois Street, Sheung Wan; tel: 2517 8484; $$
Italian restaurant serving antipasti, salads, pizza, pasta and foccacia on the corner of Jervois Street and Bonham Strand.

3

CAUSEWAY BAY
AND HAPPY VALLEY

Causeway Bay is the busiest of all Hong Kong's shopping hubs, packed with malls, stores and cafés. This tour explores its other attractions, including the green space of Victoria Park and Hong Kong's favourite sport – horse-racing.

**Mad Dogs
and Englishmen**

'In Hong Kong, they strike a gong, and fire off a noonday gun… To reprimand each inmate, who's in late' – Noël Coward. The practice of firing a cannon at the stroke of noon was begun by Jardine, Matheson & Co after they set up their trading base at Causeway Bay in the 1840s. Legend has it that Jardine's firing of the gun to salute its managers whenever they returned to Hong Kong annoyed the colonial government, and they were ordered to fire it every day as a punishment. Jardine long ago moved to Central, but still runs the gun, with the Scottish flag of its founders alongside the Bauhinia, a quaint daily reminder of the area's colourful merchant history.

> **DISTANCE** 5km (3 miles)
> **TIME** Half a day
> **START** Causeway Bay MTR
> **END** Happy Valley Racecourse
> **POINTS TO NOTE**
> Start this walk around 11.30am, to be in time to catch the midday gun. Take the MTR to Causeway Bay (Exit E) and head towards the waterfront. Most of the route can be done on foot, with tram rides around Happy Valley and to get back to the MTR or Central.

To witness a real Hong Kong tradition, make sure you are at Exit E of Causeway Bay MTR station or outside Sogo Department store by 11.30am. Head north towards the harbour along East Point Road, then cut through to the east side of the World Trade Centre. Look out for the entrance to the Centre's underground car park, and signs for the Noon-Day Gun. These will lead you under the main road through the car park, a route shared with the Police Officers' Club and the Royal Hong Kong Yacht Club. Emerge into the daylight beside the harbour, and you'll see a small garden containing the celebrated **Noon-Day Gun** ❶. As you wait for

the brief ceremony of firing the gun, take in the view of Kowloon and the contrasts of **Causeway Bay Typhoon Shelter**, which houses a mixed bag of yacht club members' luxury cruisers, rickety wooden junks and sampans. This area of water will be reclaimed temporarily during the construction of the Central-Wan Chai bypass and returned to the community in 2020.

THE PARK AND TIN HAU

After the big bang, wander east along the waterfront and cross to **Victoria Park** ❷ *(see feature p.38)*, the city's largest urban green space, and wander down to its southeast corner. This area, known as **Tin Hau** and part of North Point district, had a massive influx of residents and businesses from Shanghai

> ## Food and Drink
> ① **LES ARTISTES CAFÉ**
> 1/F Man Hoi Bldng, 98 Electric Road, North Point; tel: 3426 8918; $–$$
> Mellow café and art gallery (with a bookshop above), with pan-European food based on fresh ingredients, and exhibits by HK artists on the walls. Home-made cakes are a speciality, and it's a very relaxing spot.

in the 1950s. If you need refreshments and want to explore the urban landscape, head east along Electric Road to find **Les Artistes**, see ⑪①.

Otherwise, cross over Causeway Road to reach Tin Hau MTR station and the temple that gave it its name. Perched on a granite ledge that once overlooked the

original Causeway Bay, this **Tin Hau Temple ❸** is only the best known of more than 100 temples around the Territory dedicated to the Daoist Queen of Heaven, goddess of the sea and protector of seafarers, who is honoured by colourful celebrations on her birthday in April or May. This temple dates from

Above from far left: apartment blocks in Causeway Bay; crowd studying the form at the races; commuter heading for Happy Valley; Tin Hau Temple.

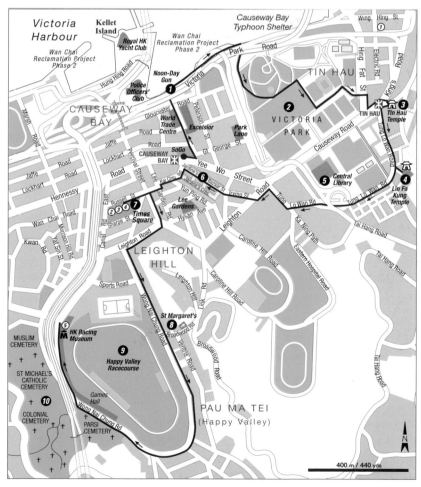

Above from left:
the course by night;
racing to the last.

Rugby Sevens
Hong Kong Stadium,
south of Victoria Park,
is the venue for the
Hong Kong Rugby
Sevens in early March.
A boisterous event,
it involves three days
of heavy drinking, silly
hats and manic singing.
See www.hksevens.
com for information.

A more cultured
event can be seen
nearby during the Mid-
Autumn Festival,
when the Tai Hang Fire
Dragon dance takes
over the quiet district
of Tin Hau. A hundred
men carry a 'dragon'
of smoking joss sticks
through the streets.

the 18th century; it has exquisite decorative details and shrines to the Azure Dragon and White Tiger, beyond the moon gates in the covered courtyard.

Lin Fa Kung Temple

Walk back down Tin Hau Temple Road and turn left into Tung Lo Wan Road to reach **Lin Fa Kung Temple** ❹ (daily 7.30am–5pm; free), set back down a lane. Dating from 1864, but renovated in 1999, it is dedicated to the Goddess of Mercy, and consists of an octagonal structure straddling a giant boulder, making it one of Hong Kong's most unusual Buddhist shrines. Inside, there's a main shrine, and a turtle pool. Climb the wooden staircase to the upper level, where you should be able to make out the shadowy silhouette of a dragon on the ceiling through the incense smoke; this

may be a reference to the Tai Hang Fire Dragon dance *(see margin left)*.

Central Library

Return to Tung Lo Wan Road, and carry on round towards the back of the sand-yellow **Central Library** ❺. Behind its Neoclassical façade is a modern 10-storey facility, with free internet access and over 4,000 journals from around the world.

CAUSEWAY SHOPPING

It's now time to explore the area with some of the most expensive retail space on the planet – but still with bargains to find. From the library, follow Tung Lo Wan Road to Leighton Road, and take the footbridge across it to Irving Street and the start of **Jardine's Bazaar** ❻, so-called because it was once a popular clothes market, although it now has a more standard mix of shops and cafés. If you take the first small alley on your left, you will find the parallel **Jardine's Crescent**, packed with shops and stalls selling cheap clothes and accessories.

Mall Life

At the end of the bazaar turn left on Kai Chiu Road to Lee Garden Road, home to bargain factory-outlet clothing shops, then cross Percival Street and its tramlines to **Times Square** ❼, one of the most glitzy of Causeway Bay's high-rise malls, with its own MTR entrance and some highly rated restaurants in the **Food Forum** on the upper floors, where you can end the tour, break for lunch, or ride the bubble lift up to see the view.

Victoria Park

Victoria Park is at its best in the early morning, when hundreds of tai chi devotees practise their graceful movements. The centre of the park is dominated by a statue of Queen Victoria: for one week each year, leading up to Chinese New Year, she's surrounded by a giant flower market, selling lucky peach blossoms and mini-orange trees. In summer, the outdoor swimming pools offer respite from the heat, and the park also has public tennis courts and a tennis stadium, which hosts major international tournaments. It's also the best place in Hong Kong to witness the mid-autumn festival lantern display.

Mall dining is a very fashionable part of the Hong Kong lifestyle, and has to be tried at least once. **WasabiSabi**, see ⑪②, and **Simply Thai**, ⑪③, are just two of the stars of the main Food Forum; alternatively, for something more laid-back and less pricey, head down to the basement food court and the **City'super Cooked Deli**, see ⑪④.

RIDE THE TRAM

After lunch, hop on a tram going south along Percival Street; get a seat upstairs to make the most of the view. As the tram rumbles along Wong Nai Chung Road, notice the elegant façade of **St Margaret's Church** ❽, perched up the hill on the left, and Happy Valley Racecourse on your right. From the end of the line, walk down along the west side of the racecourse.

HAPPY VALLEY

Happy Valley was mosquito-ridden marshland until the 1840s, when it was reclaimed by the British first for cemeteries and then, from 1846, as the spot for Hong Kong's racetrack. These days the atmosphere inside and outside the **Happy Valley Racecourse** ❾ for the Wednesday evening races (September–June) is electric; Hong Kongers love to gamble, and the Hong Kong Jockey Club is their only legal outlet. The **Hong Kong Racing Museum** (tel: 2966 8065; Tue–Sun 10am–5pm; free), in the Happy Valley Stand, tells the story in full and offers a superb view of the track, which can also be enjoyed

through the huge glass windows of **Moon Koon**, see ⑪⑤.

The Cemeteries

Across Wong Nai Chung Road are Hong Kong's oldest **cemeteries** ❿ (daily 8am–6pm). The **Parsi Cemetery** is the most picturesque, with its lush greenery. Older headstones in the **Colonial Cemetery** tell of early settlers' often youthful deaths, while Portuguese memorials in **St Michael's Catholic Cemetery** highlight links with Macau. The **Muslim** and **Jewish** cemeteries reflect other aspects of the colony's mix. When you're ready, catch a tram back to Wan Chai or Causeway Bay, or a bus south to Stanley or Aberdeen.

Grave Visits

On one day in spring (Ching Ming) and one in autumn (Cheung Yeung) families visit cemeteries and graves around the territory to pay their respects to their ancestors. They clean or 'sweep' the graves, make offerings and burn 'hell money' and gifts such as houses, furniture, mobile phones and iPods – all made out of paper.

Food and Drink

② WASABISABI
13/F Times Square, 1 Matheson Street, Causeway Bay; tel: 2526 0009; $$$
Über-cool Japanese restaurant. Enjoy their creative presentation of sushi, sashimi and other Japanese dishes with a twist, or sample sake cocktails at the sleek bar.

③ SIMPLY THAI
11/F Times Square, 1 Matheson Street, Causeway Bay; tel: 2506 1212; $$$
Relaxed contemporary restaurant that does beautifully presented dishes with fresh twists on Thai cuisine. Inspiration comes especially from Northern Thailand.

④ CITY'SUPER COOKED DELI
Basement Food Court, Times Square, 1 Matheson Street, Causeway Bay; www.citysuper.com.hk; $–$$
Top-quality fast-food counters that cover every taste – Indian, Korean, Cantonese, French patisserie, international desserts.

⑤ MOON KOON
2/F Happy Valley Stand, Wong Nai Chung Road; tel: 2966 7111; $$$
Dine out on classic Cantonese dishes at the racetrack. Barbecue buffets and a special set menu are available on race nights.

HOLLYWOOD ROAD

*A walk along Hollywood Road from its Sheung Wan origins to its new role
as the entry point to fashionable SoHo, encompassing temples, a backstreet
flea market and a huge choice of antiques shops and art galleries.*

DISTANCE 2km (1¼ mile)
TIME 2 to 3 hours
START Hollywood Road Park
END Pottinger Street, SoHo
POINTS TO NOTE

From The Landmark in Central, bus
no. 10 to Kennedy Town stops at the
Sheung Wan Civic Centre just before
Possession Street. From here, it's a
pretty easy walk, with a few steep
climbs up and down.

Below: figurines,
Chairman Mao
memorabilia and
Bruce Lee posters,
Cat Street.

HOLLYWOOD ROAD PARK

Hollywood Road is the centre of the
art and antiques trade in Hong Kong,
a winding thoroughfare lined with
dozens of shops selling all manner of
bits and pieces from the oriental past,
from period furniture to Mao memorabilia. Start your walk at **Possession
Street** where the Royal Navy landed in
1841 to claim Hong Kong Island in
the name of Queen Victoria.

Walk up the hill to join Hollywood

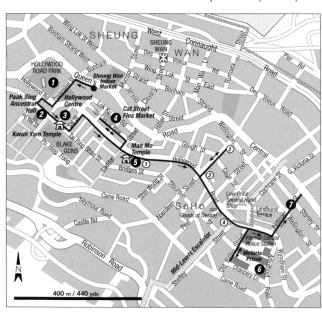

Road. On the left of the junction is the Hollywood Centre, a small arcade packed with ceramics and furniture shops. The Asian Art Archive (www.aaa.org.hk) is located on the 11th floor.

Turn right, and cross the street, where, juxtaposed with new restaurants, serviced apartments and modern galleries, you still find traditional coffin makers. **Hollywood Road Park** ❶ with its Chinese gateway still provides the living with a pleasant spot to while away their free time. Old sepia photos on the notice board show how the area looked in the early 19th century.

Paak Sing Hall

Cross to the south side of Hollywood Road, where trendy Po Yan Street leads to **Tai Ping Shan Street**. Here, the legendary pirate Cheung Po Tsai settled after receiving amnesty from the Qing emperor, some 30 years before the British arrived. Notice the tiny earth god shrines on street corners. Just to the right is **Paak Sing** ('100 Names') **Ancestral Hall** ❷, founded in 1856 to house the ancestor tablets that Hong Kong's settlers brought with them from the mainland. There are several thousand wooden tablets inside, and a variety of shrines.

Temple of Mercy

Follow Tai Ping Shan Street east; a shrine on the left and a vividly coloured temple further on are both dedicated to **Kwun Yam** ❸ (or Guanyin), Goddess of Mercy. Turn left down Sai Street to get back to Hollywood Road.

CAT STREET

Make a detour left down **Ladder Street** – made up of broad stone steps – then turn left again into **Upper Lascar Row**, home to the bustling 'Cat Street' ❹ flea market. No one can agree on the origin of this name. Some say cat burglars and pirates fenced their spoils here; others that street peddlers are known as 'cats' and their wares as 'mouse goods' in Chinese; still others claim that it's a reference to prostitutes. All are plausible, as this was once the heart of a crowded slum, notorious for opium dens, gambling parlours and brothels. What is certain is that people have been trading antiques and second-hand goods here for 150 years.

Back on Hollywood Road is one of the island's oldest temples, the **Man Mo** ❺ (c.1842), dedicated to the gods of Literature and War; the latter, appropriately, also guards over antiques dealers. A heady smell of incense wafts around the temple from dozens of giant spiralling coils of incense hanging from the ceiling that are kept constantly burning to feed the spirits.

Just around the corner at **The Press Room**, see 🍴①, you can relax at a

Tea-Time
Pause for a cup of restorative tea at the open-fronted Chinese herbal tea shop at 60 Hollywood Road.

Food and Drink 🍴

① THE PRESS ROOM
108 Hollywood Road, Central; tel: 2525 3444; $$–$$$
High-end casual dining in a modern brasserie: a New York chef's twist on classic European brasserie fare. Daily specials are marked up on a blackboard, oysters are always available, and great snacks and weekend brunches are specialities.

Above from left: shopping for antiques; night out in SoHo.

stylish brasserie with a gourmet deli-café, **Classified**, attached.

MOVING UPMARKET

Continuing east along Hollywood Road you will pass dozens of antiques shops filled with furniture, ceramics and objets d'art. When it's time for refreshments to review your finds, there are plenty of options in **SoHo** (from **So**uth of **Ho**llywood Road, though it now extends either side). A detour left down Aberdeen Street will lead to a kind of

Above: delightful dim sum; tables at The Press Room *(see p.41).*

Quality Control
Look out for shops displaying a gold *Q* sign, which means it is a member of the HK Tourist Board's Quality Tourism Scheme. For a list of QTS-accredited outlets, pick up a copy of HKTB's *A Guide to Quality Shops.*

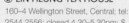

Food and Drink 🍴

② LIN HEUNG TEA HOUSE
160–4 Wellington Street, Central; tel: 2544 2556; closed 4.30–5.30pm; $
If you want an authentic yum cha experience, this is it: always busy, with relentless noise, no English signs or menus and communal round tables. Fresh dim sum is served 6am–3.30pm – you just stop passing trolleys, open the bamboo steamers and point to what you want. Dinner, served till 11pm, is Cantonese comfort food.

③ SONG
L/G 75 Hollywood Road, Central; tel: 2559 0997; $$
Nip down the alley beside 69 Hollywood Road to find Song, known for its excellent contemporary Vietnamese food. At around HK$100, the healthy buffet lunch is pretty good value. Romantic for dinner.

④ BACAR
G/F 2 Shelley Street, Soho, Central, Hong Kong; tel: 3110 1222; $$$
Two-storey Bacar hits the spot with its tapas, wines and friendly service. Food is mainly Spanish with some other Mediterranean favourites.

monument, the **Lin Heung**, see 🍴②, one of the best traditional tea and dim sum houses, and on Hollywood Road itself is Vietnamese **Song**, see 🍴③.

You can also rummage for relics and old photos of Hong Kong at the **Low Price Second Hand Shop**, an open-fronted bric-a-brac shop on the corner of Lyndhurst Terrace, or find an ironic take on Hong Kong culture at **GOD** (Goods of Desire), across the road. The Mid-Levels Escalator crosses Hollywood Road here and heads up Shelley Street. **Bacar**, see 🍴④, is a good place to stop off. (Alternatively, head up the hill for SoHo, *see opposite*, which is peppered with bars and restaurants.)

Art galleries and antiques shops start giving way to boutiques and restaurants on the remaining part of Hollywood Road. The imposing buildings across the street are the former **Central Police Station** and **Victoria Prison** ❻. The earliest of these monuments to colonial law and order were built in 1864, and new buildings were added over 60 years. Now declared 'monuments of Hong Kong', their future use is under discussion. Climb steep **Old Bailey Street** to take in the view of the former prison.

Wyndham and Pottinger Streets
Beyond the police station Hollywood Road becomes **Wyndham Street** *(see p.44)* at the top of **Pottinger Street** ❼. Named after the first governor of Hong Kong, the latter's Chinese name is far simpler – stone step street. Head east along Wyndham Street, Hong Kong's newest dining zone, or walk down Pottinger Street back to Queen's Road.

LAN KWAI FONG, WYNDHAM STREET AND SOHO

The concentration of bars and restaurants in this area of Central – where Hong Kong plays hard – makes it easy to wander around and find a venue to suit your mood.

Nightlife in Central clusters around the narrow streets and lanes in between the main business district and the Mid-Levels residential area. The two main areas, **Lan Kwai Fong** and **SoHo**, are just a short walk apart, and **Wyndham Street**, which connects the two, offers even more bars, restaurants and clubs.

Lan Kwai Fong is a small area that claims more restaurants and after-dark entertainment per block than anywhere else in Hong Kong. No longer a playground for expats-only, the 'Fong' has a clientele that's a snapshot of the international mix working and living in Hong Kong. English is spoken here, with many accents. It can all be slightly tacky, however, so if you prefer a more bohemian vibe, the relatively down-to-earth bars of SoHo should appeal.

LAN KWAI FONG

Start your night with a stroll around Lan Kwai Fong. Walk up D'Aguilar Street from Central MTR, via the signposted exit (D2). **Lan Kwai Fong ❶** itself is a short L-shaped lane that intersects the bending **D'Aguilar Street** at either end, forming a kind of square.

DISTANCE Varies *(see below)*
TIME An evening
START Central MTR, Exit D2
END Staunton and Elgin streets
POINTS TO NOTE
Since this is very much an evening stroll, with plenty of places to stop off to have a drink, a meal or just look around, the precise route is a personal choice, and the time and distance involved are entirely notional.

Below: in one of Lan Kwai Fong's numerous hip bars.

Foot Massages

Take a break from all the endless eating and drinking by having a foot massage. There are plenty of small parlours open til late and equally popular with men and women. Walk down Cochrane Street to Happy Foot Reflexology, 11/F Jade Centre, 98–102 Wellington Street; tel: 2544 1010.

One of Lan Kwai Fong's veteran establishments, **Post 97**, see ①, is now in its third decade and still a relaxing place to meet for dinner, drinks or a coffee; **Club 97** downstairs is a bit wilder, with a range of music nights for all interests and enthusiasms. The same company owns the prime spot for people-watching, **La Dolce Vita** (nos 9–11), an Italian-styled bar whose well-heeled clientele overflow onto the street clutching cocktails and European beers.

Head up to the top of the street, where the **Marlin** (56 D'Aguilar Street) Martini bar on the corner gamely aims for elegance, or bear right for the lively maritime-themed **Stormies** bar (46–50 D'Aguilar Street). Across the road in Lan Kwai Fong tower is the ever-popular and no-nonsense **Hong Kong Brew House**. In the

same building, **The Cavern** bar and restaurant has regular live music from tribute and cover bands.

Dining Out

When hunger pangs strike, most of the bars can serve snacks and often something larger, too. On D'Aguilar Street more international food options include **Al's Diner**'s legendary burgers, and Mexican snacks and 150 different kinds of tequila at **Agave**; or, turn down **Wing Wah Lane** ❷ for more Asian, cheap and cheerful street cafés. **Taste Good Thai** and **CoCo Nut Curry House** are both recommended.

Just across the junction from the very top of D'Aguilar Street, the **Fringe Club** *(see p.29 and p.122)* is worth investigating, whether for performances, to chill on the roof-garden, or to enjoy an exhibition in the main bar. For late-night music, back at 38–44 D'Aguilar, **Insomnia** has house bands playing covers, while in the basement the much more hip **Volar** hosts some of Hong Kong's best, most varied DJ sessions.

WYNDHAM STREET

On the way from Lan Kwai Fong to SoHo, there's a string of upscale yet relaxed venues to visit. **Wyndham Street** ❸ is home to great international-style bar-restaurants such as **Goccia**, see ⊺②, and has a boutique hotel (Hotel LKF; LKF Tower, no. 33). In the same building, you can tuck into Russian cuisine and drink vodka in an ice room at **Balalaika**, or for Scandinavian cool head upstairs for FINDS *(see*

Food and Drink

① POST 97
U/G 9 Lan Kwai Fong, Central; tel: 2186 1817; $–$$$
This stylish, relaxed venue has been in fashion since well before the 1997 handover. As well as a fine bar, it has an enjoyable international menu highlighting salads, pastas and brunch favourites, and when you feel like it it's an easy transfer to Club 97 downstairs.

② GOCCIA
G/F 73 Wyndham Street, Central; tel: 2167 8181; $$$
This Italian restaurant has a superb salad bar and also does delicious authentic Italian dishes. Downstairs is a funky modern bar; upstairs is an equally cool, calm dining room and terrace.

③ BISTRO MANCHU
33 Elgin Street, SoHo, Central; tel: 2536 9218; $$
Authentic northern Chinese cooking is served at this cosy, colourful restaurant. There are lots of intriguing-sounding Manchurian dishes both with and without chilli, plus some highly recommended lamb and delicious dumplings.

p. 116) a designer bar and restaurant with a terrace overlooking Wyndham Street and Lan Kwai Fong.

A few doors down at no. 57, **Gunga's** has been serving excellent Indian fare for over 20 years. Across the road at the Centrium building (no. 60), **Wagyu** offers a steak-heavy menu and is open to the street for relaxed dining and after-work drinks. **Dragon-i** *(see p.124)* is the destination of choice for the beautiful crowd; **Solas**, downstairs, is a more intimate music-focused venue.

SOHO

Of all the Central nightlife areas, SoHo has the most atmosphere, though it only developed as a nightlife zone after the **Mid-Levels Escalator** ❹ was completed in 1994. It spreads out from **Staunton Street** ❺, **Elgin Street**, and the streets around the Mid-Levels Escalator.

Good SoHo drinking haunts include **Staunton's** (10 Staunton Street), the *fin-de-siècle* drawing-room **Feather Boa** (no. 38) and **Club 1911** (no. 27), with a feel of old Shanghai. For dinner, take your pick of Moroccan delicacies at **Sahara Mezz Bar** (11 Elgin Street), Manchurian dishes at **Bistro Manchu**, see 🍴❸, also on Elgin Street, the lively **Peak Café Bar** (no. 9–13) and vegetarian **Life** (no. 10; *see p.117)*, both situated beside the escalator on Shelley Street, or dozens of other global cuisines on offer in the area.

Above from far left: spilling onto the streets of Lan Kwai Fong; chic bar on Wyndham Street.

Funky Shopping
SoHo is also home to some cute boutiques and shops selling clothes, homeware, jewellery, vintage clothes and accessories. Many are run by young designers and sell unique one-off pieces.

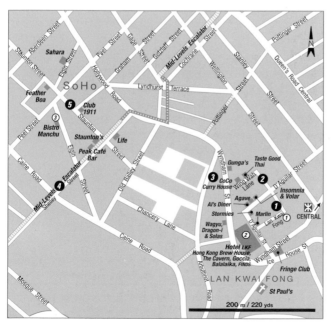

WAN CHAI AFTERNOON

Explore the backstreets, markets and temples of old Wan Chai, then head for the harbour and the spectacular new waterfront, a gleaming symbol of post-colonial Hong Kong built on reclaimed land.

Regeneration

Johnston Road and Queen's Road East are at the heart of a 10-year urban-renewal programme, which has sparked interest in Wan Chai's heritage. A number of old-style streets, such as Lee Tung Street, once home to specialist printing shops, no longer exist; other streets, including Tai Yuen Street, have been saved. After protests, Wan Chai's former indoor market, Queen's Road East, built in 1937 in the Streamline Moderne style, will become a shopping centre. Tai Wong Street and most of Cross Street market are likely to remain, surrounded by shiny new skyscrapers.

DISTANCE 3.5km (2¼ miles)
TIME 2–3 hours
START Wan Chai MTR
END Wan Chai Ferry Pier
POINTS TO NOTE
This route divides into two parts: old Wan Chai and the commercial area and giant arts and exhibition venues north of Gloucester Road. Exploring this area means walking along many pedestrian bridges and walkways: figuring them out is a distinctive Hong Kong experience.

Food and Drink

① INTERNATIONAL CURRY HOUSE

G/F 26–39 Tai Wong Street East, Wan Chai; tel: 2529 0088; $$
Small neighbourhood café that has been serving up curries from across South and East Asia for three decades. Food is as spicy as you like, from mild Malaysian satays and coconut-rich laksa to vindaloos.

② WORLD PEACE CAFÉ

21–3 Tai Wong Street East, Wan Chai; tel: 2507 5870; $
This organic and vegetarian café run by a Buddhist organisation doubles as a meditation centre, and is largely staffed by volunteers. Stop by for healthy lunch sets, juices and lassis.

OLD WAN CHAI

From Wan Chai MTR (Exit A3, on O'Brien Road), cross over the Johnston Road tramlines, and then proceed down **Tai Yuen Street** ❶, which, together with some of the neighbouring side streets, still retains much of the flavour of old Hong Kong. Walk east through the bustling street markets of **Cross Street** and **Wan Chai Road**, then cross Queen's Road East, and walk up **Stone Nullah Lane**, looking out for the **Blue House** at no. 72 (closed to visitors), a 1920s tenement building with wooden staircases and metal balconies. Almost at the end of the lane, shaded by trees, is the **Pak Tai Temple** ❷ (1860s), surrounded by trees, which contains a 3m (10ft) copper statue of the Daoist god Pak Tai that is said to be over 400 years old.

The First Waterfront

Retrace your steps to **Queen's Road East**, which marks Wan Chai's original waterfront. It is now best known for soft furnishings stores and shops selling traditional rattan and rosewood furniture. Head west as far as the former **Wan Chai Post Office** ❸ (1912), on the corner of Wan Chai Gap Road. This quaint whitewashed building served as

the district's post office until 1992; nowadays it houses the **Environmental Resource Centre** (Wed–Mon 10am–5pm; free). Take a look inside at the original wooden counter and red postboxes; nature lovers can also pick up a leaflet on the 1.5km (1-mile) **Wan Chai Green Trail**, which starts at the 80-year-old mango and giant candlenut trees just outside, and from very urban beginnings climbs up into the steep, thickly wooded hillsides to the south.

TOWERS AND TEMPLES

Now head west to the circular 66-storey **Hopewell Centre ❹**, the tallest building in town in the 1980s, and ride the glass-bubble lift for some of the city's most spectacular views. In its shadow, to the west, is the **Hung Shing (Tai Wong) Temple ❺**, from 1860. You can smell the incense before you see it. As befits its former waterfront location, the temple is dedicated to one of the patron gods of fishermen. Notice the boulders incorporated into its design, and the sacred banyan tree behind it.

Tai Wong Street

Cross back over Queen's Road East and walk down **Tai Wong Street East ❻**, a characteristically eclectic Wan Chai street, with tea shops and a clutch of restaurants, including the popular **International Curry House** and a meditation centre that also hosts the **World Peace Café**, see ⑪① and ②. At no. 20 is the picturesque old **Woo Cheong Pawn Shop**, with distinctive tall counters inside.

Note that round the corner, Johnston Road is a good place to stop for some bargain hunting at the jostling factory outlets. At no. 62, are three century-old shophouses, which have been beautifully restored and converted into **The Pawn** restaurant *(see p.119)*.

Continue the route, though, along Luard Road, which runs north from

Above from far left: egg seller; Hung Shing Temple; Golden Forever-Blooming Bauhinia; the sail of a junk in front of the Hong Kong Convention and Exhibition Centre.

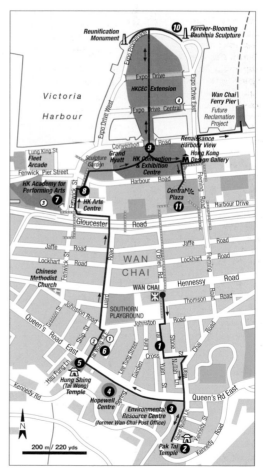

the junction of Tai Wong Street and Johnston Road. This street is the heart of Wan Chai's nightlife district, covered in full in the next tour *(see pp.50–3)*.

RECLAMATION

When you reach the multi-lane Gloucester Road, take any pedestrian bridge across, towards the amazing imposing towers of the Inland Revenue and Immigration. These skyscrapers built on reclaimed land form the 'new' Wan Chai, a concentration of huge buildings linked by a web of pedestrian bridges.

To the left is the **Hong Kong Academy for Performing Arts (APA)** ❼ *(see p.122)*, a college of dance, music and drama that doubles as a performance venue. To the right in Harbour Road is the **Hong Kong Arts Centre** ❽, dedicated to contemporary art and culture, with galleries, a theatre, a cinema, a shop and the **Pumpernickel Café**, see ⑪③.

Above: quirky contemporary design at the Hong Kong Arts Centre.

The Convention Centre

Leave the Arts Centre by the footbridge on the second floor, and cross over Harbour Road. The first stairway to the right leads down through a small sculpture garden and enters the impressive lobby of the **Grand Hyatt** hotel. The stairs on the right lead into the **Hong Kong Convention and Exhibition Centre (HKCEC)** ❾. This building first opened in 1988, but an extension on a reclaimed semi-'island' built into the harbour more than doubled its size; the extension was completed in 1997, just in time for it to serve as the venue for the historic Handover Ceremony on 30 June, when China resumed sovereignty. Such is the demand for exhibition space in Hong Kong that a second expansion was completed in 2009. Take the escalator into the new building, and walk through its many corridors and open spaces towards the harbour.

The Golden Bauhinia

Leave the complex at the Expo Drive entrance, and walk along **Expo Promenade** for dramatic views of the Harbour and Kowloon. This is a favourite photo-opportunity spot for mainland Chinese tourists, who like to pose by the black **Reunification Monument**, commemorating the 1997 handover, and by the golden **Forever-Blooming Bauhinia** ❿ sculpture. The elegant orchid-like bauhinia is an indigenous flower and Hong Kong's emblem; its five petals appear on the territory's red-and-white flag and on coins.

Food and Drink

③ PUMPERNICKEL CAFÉ
4/F Hong Kong Arts Centre, 2 Harbour Road, Wan Chai; tel: 2588 1001; $
This is an ideal place to research arts events while taking in the view. Home-made breads, pastries and sandwiches plus great coffee and some substantial lunch set menus add to the appeal.

④ CONGRESS RESTAURANT
6/F Convention Plaza, 1 Harbour Road, Wan Chai; tel: 2582 7250; $$$
An extensive international buffet makes Congress popular with locals and trade-fair visitors. Choose from Asian and European favourites and mountains of seafood.

If you want to linger for a while longer in this area, you can eat well and enjoy fabulous views from the floor-to-ceiling windows at the centre's **Congress restaurant**, see ⑪④.

CENTRAL PLAZA

Retrace your steps to the HKCEC's main entrance, and follow signs to the **Renaissance Harbour View** mall, where the **Hong Kong Design Gallery** (tel: 2584 4146; Mon–Fri 10am–7.30pm, Sat 10am–7pm, Sun noon–7.30pm) showcases original Hong Kong design.

Continue out through the mall and follow signs for **Central Plaza** ⑪, which rises some 78 floors to 374m (1,227ft). The Sky Lobby on the 46th floor acts a free viewing gallery (Mon–Fri 8am–7pm, Sat 8am–1pm; free), as well as a changeover spot for lifts for some of the 6,000 people who work here.

After returning to earth, follow signs back to Wan Chai MTR station or take the Star Ferry to Tsim Sha Tsui from the nearby Wan Chai Ferry Pier. Alternatively, explore Wan Chai after dark *(see pp.50–3)*.

7

WAN CHAI AFTER DARK

Buzzing after-work bars, clubs, cinemas, music and arts venues and restaurants of all sorts vie with the sleazy girlie-bars of Suzie Wong fame. Mix your own Wan Chai cocktail, and join one of the best parties in town.

DISTANCE Varies

TIME All night

START Wan Chai MTR

END Star Street

POINTS TO NOTE

This route easily breaks down into three parts. Everywhere in Wan Chai is accessible by tram, bus or MTR, and ferries run to Tsim Sha Tsui from near the Convention Centre. If you make a night of it, taxis are plentiful.

Where to Go in Wan Chai

Sanlitun is ideal for couples and mixed groups to dine, off the main drag with a lively, mainly local, after-work crowd. The Lockhart Road area is where people really let their hair down – more of a raucous stag- and hen-night vibe. Star Street is a cool, chic hang-out with prices to match.

Even 50 years on, Wan Chai is still inveterately linked with Richard Mason's 1957 novel *The World of Suzie Wong*, and the 1960 film version starring William Holden and Nancy Kwan. Today, it offers a far more eclectic mix of night-time entertainment than it did in its heyday as a raunchy retreat for US servicemen during the Korean and Vietnam wars. Hostess bars have been eclipsed by trendy ones, and there is an increasingly thriving restaurant scene.

ARTS AND MUSIC

The remorseless **Wan Chai Reclamation**, snatching land away from Victoria Harbour, has provided land for hotels, malls, offices and dazzling arts and exhibition venues in an area sometimes referred to as North Wan Chai. Along with the City Hall in Central and the Cultural Centre on the Tsim Sha Tsui waterfront, this is one of Hong Kong's foremost areas for live performances of all kinds. Even today's waterfront is temporary, as the final phase, complete with a major new bypass and rail link, is due to be completed by 2020.

If you're a fan of contemporary art, theatre or a film buff, begin by leaving Wan Chai MTR at Exit C and walking down Luard Road to see what's on at the harbourfront **Hong Kong Arts Centre** ❶ (tel: 2582 0200; www.hkac. org.hk). Just nearby, the **Hong Kong Academy of Performing Arts** ❷ (tel: 2584 8500; www.hkapa.edu) hosts local

Food and Drink

① JACK'S TERRAZA

Shop 8, 1/F Sanlitun Causeway Centre, 28 Harbour Road, Wan Chai; tel: 2827 1687; $$

Sample the atmosphere of bustling Sanlitun's dozen or more restaurants by dining alfresco on the terrace. Nothing too fancy at Jack's – just pasta, pizza, steaks and seafood.

② DUETTO

2/F Sun Hung Kai Centre, 30 Harbour Road, Wan Chai; tel: 2827 7777; $$$

A popular upmarket Indian restaurant merged with its Italian sister next door to create Duetto, which offers a cross-continental menu from its huge open kitchen. The terrace, which has panoramic views, is great for happy-hour drinks. Punchline Comedy Club (in English), with international comedians, is held here once a month.

and visiting theatre companies, concerts by both its own students and international musicians, and even productions of Broadway and West End musicals. Biggest of all, the **Hong Kong Convention and Exhibition Centre** ❸ (tel: 2582 8888; www.hkcec.com) is a frequent venue for big-name international rock and pop acts.

Food for Thought

Wan Chai's waterfront has a few elegant options for dining and socialising hidden away. The **Grand Hyatt** hotel, on one side of the Convention Centre, has two of Hong Kong's most acclaimed restaurants, **Grissini** (top-notch Italian) and **One Harbour Road** (refined Can-

tonese), both combining sensational harbour views and glamour. The Hyatt's **Champagne Bar** is also one of the most classily opulent drinking spots in town.

For a more low-key (and cheaper) evening, you could combine a show with a meal at **Jack's Terraza**, see ⑪①, or anywhere in the nearby **Sanlitun Causeway Centre** ❹. Next to it, the **Sun Hung Kai Centre** ❺ offers a choice of sophisticated restaurants with great harbour views. **Duetto** has outdoor seating and offers a modern combination of Indian and Italian fare, see ⑪②. It's also the long-standing venue for the **Punchline Comedy Club**, which brings international stand-up stars to Hong Kong each month.

Above from far left: ready for a theatrical night; celebrations in Wan Chai.

Below: Wan Chai neon.

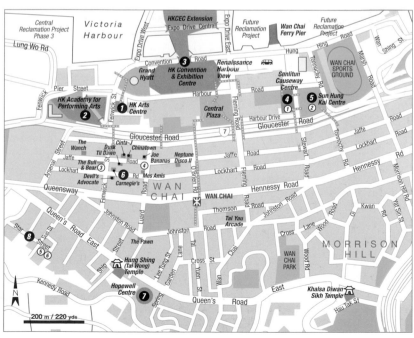

Above from left: well-stocked Wan Chai bar; neon-lit Lockhart Road.

GLOBAL CHOICES

To make a night of it after eating, you don't need to look far either. From the Convention Centre area, find your way through the pedestrian bridges over Gloucester Road, and head up Luard Road. There is an apparently endless choice of places to eat: local institutions such as the (North Chinese) **American Restaurant**, see ⑪③, or colonial-style-Indian **Jo Jo Mess** at 86–90 Johnston Road, but also stylish arrivals such as **Uno Más** (54–62 Lockhart Road). You can have inexpensive Burmese (**Golden Myanmar**, 379–89 Jaffe Road) or British pub grub (**The Bull & Bear**, 52–8 Jaffe Road).

Cinta-J (69 Jaffe Road) has enjoyable Filipino-Indonesian-Malaysian food, then becomes a cocktail lounge as the night runs on. Of Wan Chai's drinking spots, **Delaney's**, see ⑪④, is a reliable landmark.

WONG'S WORLD

The boisterous, nonstop hub of Wan Chai nightlife is still in the same place that it was in the Suzie Wong era – although today you can no longer step out from here straight onto the waterfront, as you could in her day. It's centred on **Lockhart Road** ❻ and **Jaffe Road**, above all where they cross **Luard Road** and **Fenwick Street**. There are no longer many sailors around, nor even many black-curtained girlie bars with morose doormen. Instead, the area is packed with a colourful mix of bars, restaurants and all-night clubs. Compared to the more sharp-and-stylish parts of Hong Kong, the atmosphere is laid-back, unfussy, prices are fairly pain-free, and it rivals Lan Kwai Fong as a spot for Hong Kong's multinational population to let its hair down.

MUSIC AND DANCING

If you want to hear some live music, check out tiny, down-to-earth **The Wanch** (54 Jaffe Road) or **Carnegie's** (53–5 Lockhart Road), a downhome American bar with excellent music and a party vibe: dancing on the bar is common but not compulsory. For a bit more space, **Devil's Advocate** (48–50 Lockhart Road) is a lively sports bar,

Food and Drink 🍴

③ AMERICAN RESTAURANT

G/F 20 Lockhart Road, Wan Chai; tel: 2527 7277; $$
Don't let the name fool you: the 'American' has been serving tasty Northern Chinese food (great Peking duck) – for over 50 years.

④ DELANEY'S

G-1/F One Capital Place, 18 Luard Road, Wan Chai; tel: 2804 2880; $$
Always-buzzing Irish pub and sports bar with football, rugby and more sports on a big screen upstairs, and a quieter bar below. Guinness on tap, and excellent, hearty food.

⑤ CINECITTA

9 Star Street, Wan Chai; tel: 2529 0199; $$$
This stunning Roman restaurant, designed by Tony Chi, presents a delectable choice of modern Italian cuisine. The bar serves complimentary canapés during happy hour (6–9pm).

⑥ 1/5 NUEVO

Starcrest Building, 9 Star Street, Wan Chai; tel: 2529 2300; $$
'One-Fifth Nuevo' is the hub of the new smarter Wan Chai scene. It's a two-storey, very hip, high-ceilinged bar, with casual dining and Spanish-inspired food. The bar eases effortlessly into an ever-so-cool club as the night goes on.

while **Mes Amis** at 83 Lockhart Road is a great people-watching spot that changes from French wine bar to wild dance bar late-night.

For something wilder, **Joe Bananas** (23 Luard Road) is one of Wan Chai's most fun, full-on, old-fashioned discos. And for carrying on till sunrise, head for **Dusk Til Dawn** (76 Jaffe Road) with cover bands, or the more sleazy **Neptune Disco II** (98–108 Jaffe Road). Both will carry you through till after 7am – just don't expect anything too cutting-edge.

STAR STREET

Finding the more upmarket nightlife scene in Wan Chai means heading for the older part of the district, located to the south of Johnston Road. There are plenty more restaurants: you can spin while you dine on international cuisine at the **R66** revolving restaurant on the 62nd (not 66th) floor of the **Hopewell Centre** ❼, reached by a swish glass-bubble lift.

To discover the most fashionable spot hereabouts, though, head west along Queen's Road East to Wing Fung Street, then turn left up it to **Star Street** ❽, a short lane that has recently become one of Hong Kong's style enclaves. There are shops, cafés and, above all, bar-restaurants such as **Cinecitta** and **1/5 Nuevo**, see ⑪⑤ and ⑥, which meet the needs of a cool clientele, serving exquisite food and excellent cocktails amid sleek modern elegance.

Tea with Style
Before trying any of Star Street's more buzzing venues, get properly mellow at Ming Cha (7 Star Street). An attractive contemporary variation on the traditional Chinese tea shop, it has over 40 varieties of the finest-quality Chinese teas (mostly Oolong), which you can buy to take away or sample at the tea bar (noon–9pm).

Below: still from the film of *The World of Suzie Wong*.

VICTORIA PEAK

It's a natural reaction to Hong Kong's urban intensity: residents and visitors alike feel the need to ride up the Peak on its famous tram to get a full view of the architectural forest and explore the city's green mountain.

Above: at Madame Tussaud's; pagoda on the Peak.

DISTANCE 4km (2½ miles)
TIME Half to a full day
START/END Peak Tram Lower Terminus, Garden Road, Central
POINTS TO NOTE
To reach the Peak Tram's starting point on Garden Road, walk up from Admiralty MTR through Hong Kong Park (this should take approximately 10 mins) or take bus 15C from the Central Ferry Piers via Connaught Road. Trams run daily, 7am to midnight, and around every 15 mins.

One of the world's steepest funicular railways, the **Peak Tram ❶** has been running since 1888, and is one of Hong Kong's must-do rides. Its spectacular eight-minute ascent does not end at the summit of Victoria Peak but at the base of the 1997 **Peak**

Tower ❷, at a height of 373m (1,223ft). Designed by British architect Terry Farrell in the shape of an upheld rice bowl, the seven-storey complex is topped by the **Sky-Terrace** (Mon–Fri 10am–11pm, Sat, Sun and public holidays 8am–11pm), from where there are stunning 360-degree views of Hong Kong at 428m (1,404ft) above sea level.

In the Tower

Indoor attractions include state-of-the-art virtual reality rides and interactive games at the **EA Experience**, and **Madame Tussaud's** (charges for both), where you can pose with wax effigies of both Western and Asian celebrities. Throughout the Tower there are plenty of places to eat, snack, admire the view, and find the ultimate Hong Kong souvenir. Dining options range from refined Japanese or Cantonese cuisine and the elegant **Pearl on the Peak** *(see p.30)* to juice bars and theme restaurants such as the Forrest Gump-inspired **Bubba Gump Shrimp Co**, see ⑪①.

Across the road from the Tower is the **Peak Galleria ❸**, less architecturally spectacular but with four floors of smart shops and restaurants, and a viewing platform. Also nearby is one of the most relaxing places to take in the view, the **Peak Lookout** *(see p.30)*.

Food and Drink 🍴

① BUBBA GUMP SHRIMP CO
Level 3, The Peak Tower; tel: 2849 2867; $$
All-American theme restaurant serving up huge portions of shrimp, plus Southern-style dishes, smoothies and Forrest's favourite puds.

② CAFÉ DECO
Level 1–2, Peak Galleria, 118 Peak Road; tel: 2849 5111; $$–$$$
An eclectic fusion menu strong on seafood, steaks and Thai influences, with live jazz most evenings and fabulous city views.

AROUND THE PEAK

Walk south from the Peak Tower (ie away from the view) into **Lugard Road**, the start of a gentle circular walk around Victoria Peak, which takes about an hour to complete. The tree-lined path winds past isolated colonial villas that rank among the most expensive and exclusive homes in the territory, a world apart from the high-rise metropolis below. On clear days (increasingly rare) you can see beyond the harbour and Kowloon to the Nine Dragon Ridge, which separates urban Hong Kong from the New Territories, and across to the hills stretching up to Shenzhen. Pause to watch the black kites float on thermal currents above the city, and the hundreds of ships in the harbour.

Lugard Road merges with **Harlech Road** ❹ at a four-path junction and shaded picnic spot. The path winds east along the thickly wooded southern flank of the mountain back to the Peak

Tower and the tram stop. It's a popular jogging and exercise circuit.

Up to the Top

Pause for refreshment at the Peak Lookout, then, if you're feeling sufficiently energetic, continue on up **Mt Austin Road** – watching out for speeding cars – which after a steep 20-minute walk runs out at the actual summit of **Victoria Peak** ❺, at 552m (1,811ft). On the way, make a detour into **Victoria Peak Gardens** ❻, for more elevated views and greenery. A path, the **Governor's Walk**, runs around the well-tended gardens, all that remains of the early governors' summer residence. Take mosquito repellent if you plan to linger till dusk before wandering back down Mt Austin Road.

Back by the tram station, grab a drink at **Café Deco**, see ⑪②, in the Galleria, to watch the city light up as darkness settles, and have dinner there before catching a tram back downhill.

Above from far left: inside the Peak Tower; view from the Peak.

Extending the Walk

If you feel like a longer hike, there are plenty more options from the Peak. From the crossing of Lugard Road and Harlech Road (see left), another path leads down into Pokfulam Country Park, arriving after about 45 minutes' walking at Pokfulam reservoir, taking in the beautiful views. Continue on past ponies and retired racehorses at the Hong Kong Jockey Club Public Riding School to Pokfulam Road, where you can catch a bus or taxi to Central or Aberdeen; or, go further along the Hong Kong Trail, which runs for 50km (30 miles) right across Hong Kong Island. It is also possible to walk back to Central from the Peak Tower – just follow the marked paths downhill (allow around 45 minutes).

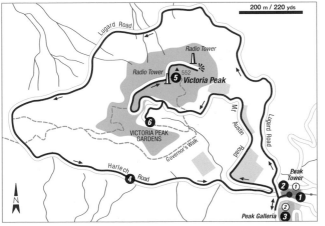

200 m / 220 yds

Lugard Road

Radio Tower

Radio Tower

552
❺ **Victoria Peak**

❻

VICTORIA PEAK GARDENS

Governor's Walk

Mt Austin Road

Lugard Road

Harlech Road

❹

Peak Tower

❷ ⑦
❶

❷
Peak Galleria ❸

N

SOUTHSIDE

Hong Kong Island's alter ego: a leisurely exploration of the still-uncrowded south shore, with the floating restaurants of Aberdeen, family fun at Ocean Park, beaches in Repulse Bay, and the seaside market town of Stanley.

Above: onto the boats at Aberdeen; apartment block in Repulse Bay.

DISTANCE 10km (6 miles)
TIME At least half a day, excluding Ocean Park
START Aberdeen
END Stanley
POINTS TO NOTE

A bus-and-walk tour: for Aberdeen, take 7 or 71 bus from the Ferry Piers bus station; from Aberdeen, then take bus 48 from Aberdeen Main Road to get to Ocean Park, or bus 73 to Repulse Bay and Stanley. Weekends and holidays are very busy, especially at Ocean Park and Stanley.

Food and Drink

① JUMBO RESTAURANT

Jumbo Kingdom, Sham Wan Pier Drive, Aberdeen; tel: 2553 9111; $$–$$$
This place trades on its reputation as a Hong Kong institution, rather than the excellent food it serves. Maybe just order a dish or two to sample the atmosphere. Large, loud, bright and kitsch.

② TOP DECK AT THE JUMBO

Jumbo Kingdom, Sham Wan Pier Drive, Aberdeen; tel: 2552 3331; $$–$$$
The highlight of many a visit to Aberdeen is a long lunch or dinner at Top Deck, followed by drinks while lounging on the sofas outside on the deck, overlooking flashy yachts and humble sampans. The decor is elegant oriental, making this a classy cousin to the loud Jumbo downstairs. The food is international, with Chinese, Japanese, Asian and European dishes and fresh imported seafood. Book ahead for weekend brunch buffet.

Within a short distance of Central, Hong Kong Island's south side offers respite from the intensely urbanised north shore. To the surprise of many visitors, much of it still consists of forested mountains, sweeping vistas, small towns and broad bays with fine beaches. The four main attractions – Aberdeen Harbour, Ocean Park, Repulse Bay and Stanley – are all easily accessible by bus. The journey is part of the fun, as there are some breathtaking views along the way as the road winds over mountains and around the coast.

ABERDEEN

Buses arrive at **Aberdeen Bus Station**. From here, take either the footbridge or subway across Aberdeen Praya Road to Hong Kong's liveliest waterfront. The promenade has lately been enhanced with trees, benches and signs with potted histories of different sights.

The Harbour

Aberdeen ❶ itself is still very much a working harbour. The attractive sight of a harbour full of fishing boats belies the fact, though, that Hong Kong waters' fish stocks are critically low after decades of overfishing. This has been a fishing port for hundreds of years, long before the British decided

to name it after their Foreign Secretary, Lord Aberdeen, in the 1840s. Its Chinese name, *Heung Kong Tsai* (Little Fragrant Harbour), is thought to allude to the port's centuries-old trade in fragrant incense wood.

At one time over 20,000 Tanka and Hoklo 'boat people' lived on traditional wooden junks in the sheltered anchorage. Most have now traded their floating homes for high-rise flats nearby, but a sizeable community remains.

Sampans and Floating Restaurants
A sampan ride through this crowded waterway is a highlight of any trip. The sampan operators (often elderly women) are always ready to negotiate a fee for an occasionally hair-raising spin between the fishing trawlers, ramshackle live-aboard junks, and pleasure craft.

Another way to take a trip through the harbour is on the free shuttle boats (signposted at points along Aberdeen waterfront) to the magnificently gaudy **Jumbo Kingdom**, see ⑪①, Aberdeen's famous 'floating restaurants', celebrated in films set in Hong Kong for over 50 years. The huge multi-deck illuminated pagodas have had a makeover recently, but the over-the-top gold dragons and the grand entrance remain the same. The Dragon Court and Jumbo Chinese restaurants are on the first and second floors, and the rooftop has been transformed into the **Top Deck**, see ⑪②, a

Above from far left: Jumbo Kingdom; small beach near Stanley; super-fresh fish at a street stall; Stanley Beach.

Shopping Detour
From Aberdeen you can take a side-trip shopping. Nearby Ap Lei Chau is the most densely populated island on earth and home to Horizon Plaza, which is full of warehouse-size stores selling furniture, home furnishings and end-of-season designer clothes.

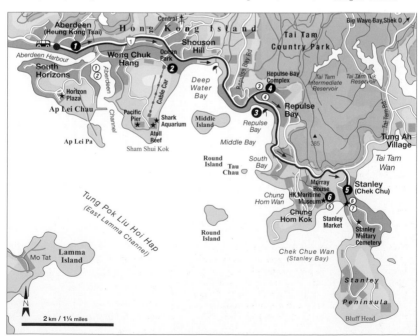

Extras at Ocean Park

Animal-lovers should book in advance for Ocean Park's behind-the-scenes programmes, which enable visitors to learn more about the park's residents. At Halloween and Christmas the park puts on spectacular extra events and extends opening until 8pm.

bar and restaurant that is a destination in itself. Boats to the Jumbos are signposted at a number of points along Aberdeen waterfront.

OCEAN PARK

Ocean Park ❷ (tel: 2552 0291, www.oceanpark.com.hk; daily 10am–6pm; entrance charge), on the peninsula east of Aberdeen, is Hong Kong's longest-running theme park and oceanarium. Despite recent competition from Disneyland *(see pp.74–5)*, it is still a local favourite, drawing over five million visitors a year, with new rides, animal attractions and three new hotels already planned. The oceanariums and spectacular cliff-top setting make it enjoyable even if theme parks usually leave you cold. Buses run direct to the park from various parts of Hong Kong.

Atolls, Rides and Pandas

Highlights of Ocean Park include the stunning **Atoll Reef**, **Shark Aquarium** and **Pacific Pier**, a 'natural' habitat for both seals and sea lions. There are also

thrills of increasing degrees, from the 72m (236ft) **observation tower** to **cable car** and escalator rides up and down the headland and the **Abyss Turbo Drop** or other hair-raising rides and roller coasters. The **Giant Panda Habitat** is home to four pandas, gifts from the Beijing government: the first pair An An and Jia Jia arrived in 1999; youngsters Le Le and Ying Ying followed in 2007 to commemorate the SAR's tenth anniversary. Allow at least four hours to explore, especially if visiting with children, as there's lots to see.

REPULSE BAY

Beyond the Ocean Park headland there open up two of the most beautiful stretches of coastline on the island, **Deep Water Bay** and **Repulse Bay ❸**. The most common theory for the latter's name is that the bay was once used as a refuge by pirates, who were 'repulsed' by the British Navy in the 1840s. It has some of the loveliest, most popular beaches in Hong Kong. It's hard to find a spare centimetre of sand on summer weekends, but the beaches are often deserted on weekdays. To get here from Ocean Park, turn right out of the main entrance and walk up to Wong Chuk Hang Road to catch the no. 73 bus from Aberdeen.

Life by the Bay

Repulse Bay became a popular relaxation spot for Hong Kong colonials in the 1920s, when the Repulse Bay Hotel was built, an architectural gem and the belle of colonial society. Over the years

---

Food and Drink 🍴

③ VERANDAH

109 Repulse Bay Road, Repulse Bay; tel: 2292 2822; $$$
An atmospheric evocation of the colonial era, with ceiling fans, palms, acres of 1930s-style woodwork and a stunning sea view. The menu is classic European, and afternoon tea and Sunday brunch are specialities. Always book for weekends.

④ Y-BY-THE-BAY

202 The Arcade, 109 Repulse Bay Road, Repulse Bay; tel: 2812 2120; $$
With tables in a garden, this modest Japanese restaurant is especially relaxing. On the menu are noodles, sushi and sashimi.

Noël Coward, George Bernard Shaw, Marlon Brando and many more famous visitors were all refreshed by the view from its famous terrace.

Sadly, most of the hotel was swept aside in 1982 to make room for the **Repulse Bay Complex ❹**, with restaurants, a fancy spa, shops and plush apartment blocks, which have helped the Bay become an even more popular residential area for wealthy locals. One, bright blue, block has a large hole in the middle, allegedly introduced by the architect for feng shui reasons – to allow the dragon that lives inside the mountain behind to get down to the sea. But nevertheless, within the complex is a new luxurious **Repulse Bay Hotel** that is a partial reconstruction of the original – incorporating parts of the old building – and has the lovely restaurant, **Verandah**, see ⑪③, which effectively recalls the old days in decor and service. It enjoys the same celebrated view as its predecessor, and is one of Hong Kong's most enjoyable brunch venues.

Life Guard Club

There are more economical eating options elsewhere near the beach, such as **Y-by-the-Bay**, see ⑪④. At the south end of the beach is the rather bizarre **Life Guard Club**, which looks more like a temple than a restaurant with its colourful collection of images, including huge statues of the Buddhist goddess Kwun Yam and her Daoist counterpart Tin Hau, both protectors of fishermen.

Surfing Hong Kong
Between them, Deep Water Bay and Repulse Bay have Hong Kong's most popular, most easily accessible beaches, with plentiful places to eat and other facilities to help you enjoy a day by the sea. The place to go for surfers in Hong Kong, though, is the suitably named Big Wave Bay, in the island's southeast corner. Boards can be hired, and there are suitably mellow places to eat and drink nearby in Shek O, one of Hong Kong island's smallest and most easy-going villages.

Left: hungry panda at the Giant Panda Habitat, Ocean Park.

Above from left:
incense and tea at a temple; multilingual signs; pictures for sale at Stanley Market; Shek O main beach.

Below: antiques at Stanley Market.

STANLEY

From Repulse Bay, catch a no. 73 bus again, or any bus marked for Stanley. The road hugs the picturesque coastline of **Chung Hom Wan** (bay), looking westward to Lamma Island. Like Aberdeen, **Stanley** ❺ was a thriving fishing village long before the British arrived. The local Hakka people named it *Chek Chue* or 'robbers' lair', because it was a haven for smugglers and pirates. Nowadays, it's a residential enclave of wealthy commuters, with a seaside-village feel. There is a choice of restaurants and a buzzing street market.

Around Stanley Market
Stanley Market (daily 11am–6pm) is a maze of stalls and little shops, just down the hill from the bus stop on Stanley Village Road. Apart from the colourful food and flower section, it caters largely to tourists and expats. Prices may not be a 'steal', but it's still

Food and Drink 🍴

❺ WILDFIRE
2/F Murray House, Stanley;
tel: 2813 6161; $$
Offering an exceptional choice of pizzas plus steaks, salads and seafood platters, Wildfire is on the top floor of beautiful Murray House. It's amply spacious, with high ceilings, a balcony, a children's play area and fine views across the bay.

❻ THE BOATHOUSE
86–88 Stanley Main Street, Stanley;
tel: 2813 4467; $$
A nautically oriented gastropub on the Stanley waterfront: tuck into seafood, salads, sandwiches, pasta, great fish and chips and other international favourites. It extends over three storeys, with a roof garden providing the best seats in the house.

❼ SHU ZHAI
80 Stanley Main Street, Stanley;
tel: 2813 0123; closed Mon; $$
This gorgeous traditional-style tea house, tucked behind the Dymocks store, is a shady retreat from the crowds. Choose between dim sum or modern Chinese cuisine, both served all day.

a great place to browse for gifts and souvenirs. Good buys include embroidered linen, silk and linen clothes, sportswear, pictures, chops *(see p.35)* and craftwork.

Head along **Stanley Main Street** past a strip of bars, bistros and pubs, and you will find a tiny **Tai Wong Temple** built into a rock, just before **Stanley Plaza**, a modern mall. On the opposite side of the plaza is a **Tin Hau Temple** that looks somewhat modern and functional, although a temple has been here since the 18th century. It houses an ancient drum and bell, dated 1767, which belonged to the legendary Qing-dynasty pirate Cheung Po-Tsai, and the rather tatty skin of Hong Kong's last wild tiger, shot in Stanley in 1942.

The temple was once on the shoreline, but nowadays the promenade is dominated by **Murray House** ⑥. Dating from 1848, this neoclassical former British officers' mess stood in Central Hong Kong until 1982, when it was taken apart piece by piece to make way for the Bank of China tower. After almost 20 years in storage, Murray House was reassembled and opened in 2001.

Situated on the ground floor is the excellent **Hong Kong Maritime Museum** (tel: 2813 2322; www.hk maritimemuseum.org; Tue–Sun 10am–6pm; free), which explores Hong Kong's long relationship with the sea. Upstairs there's a good selection of restaurants such as **Wildfire**, see ⑪⑤, where you can take a break under whirring ceiling fans or on the balconies and enjoy the view.

The Beach and Military Cemetery
Later, head back towards the market and then continue along Wong Ma Kok Road towards the secluded **St Stephen's Beach**, and the well-tended **Stanley Military Cemetery** (daily 10am–7pm; free), where colonial soldiers and World War II prisoners of war are buried.

Head back into town along Stanley Village Road, past the **former Stanley Police Station** (1859, no. 88), the territory's oldest police building, and now a supermarket. There are lots of good places for watching the sunset over Stanley Bay over drinks or dinner: as well as those in Murray House, try **The Boathouse**, see ⑪⑥, on Stanley Main Street, or, for something more Chinese, the beautiful **Shu Zhai**, see ⑪⑦. Afterwards, take the escalator through Stanley Plaza to the main road for buses back to the city.

East to Shek O
Beyond Stanley, Tai Tam Road winds its way to join Shek O Road, eventually leading to the eponymous village, and one of Hong Kong Island's best beaches. Shek O itself, accessed more directly from Central on the 309 bus, is a small residential outpost with a few good restaurants. Just to the north, Big Wave Bay is – as the name suggests – the SAR's premier surfing centre.

Tai Tam Country Park

A huge amount of Hong Kong Island, especially towards the south side, is given over to country parks; the largest is the Tai Tam, which covers most of the mountain ridge between Causeway Bay and Stanley. An oasis of green calm, it's easy to explore: take a no. 6, 61 or 66 bus from Exchange Square in Central to Parkview on Wong Nai Chung Gap Road, from where it's a fairly undemanding, downhill hike past glittering reservoirs to Tai Tam Road (about 2km/1¼ miles). From this point you can get buses back to town or to Stanley, or try a tougher walk over the 'Dragon's Back' to the laid-back village of Shek O (16km/10 miles). Alternatively, do the 'Wilson Trail' down from Wong Nai Chung Gap to Stanley (5km/3 miles), past some superb views.

10

TSIM SHA TSUI

Visit the Hong Kong Museum of Art and The Peninsula — one of the world's great hotels — then continue north to Kowloon's shopping Golden Mile, dropping in on Kowloon Park and the Hong Kong Science Museum.

DISTANCE 5.5km (3¼ miles)
TIME Half to a full day
START/END Star Ferry Pier, Tsim Sha Tsui
POINTS TO NOTE
Time your TST outing to ensure you are in a vantage spot at 8pm to catch the Symphony of Lights, the world's largest permanent sound-and-light show, which lights up the skyline of Kowloon and Hong Kong every night.

Above: Kowloon is renowed for its neon lights.

This tour will help you get your bearings around Tsim Sha Tsui, the bustling district at the tip of Kowloon peninsula. TST, as locals often call it, is known for its museums, hotels, restaurants, entertainment and the beginning of the 'Golden Mile' of Nathan Road, Kowloon's glittering and seemingly endless (certainly much longer than a mile) shopping strip.

Food and Drink

① JADE GARDEN

4/F Star House, 3 Salisbury Road, Tsim Sha Tsui;
tel: 2730 6888; $–$$

Right by Star Ferry Pier, with lovely harbour views, this is one of a local chain known for their fine traditional dim sum, served until 5pm. Don't worry if the trolleys look intimidating: there's an easy-to-use English menu. The rest of the Star House arcade is full of intriguing souvenir shops.

AROUND THE STAR FERRY

Start from Hong Kong Tourist Board's Kowloon office (daily 8am–8pm) by the **Star Ferry concourse ❶**, where TST ferries from Hong Kong Island arrive. To your left is Harbour City, a vast complex of five upscale shopping malls and the Ocean Terminal, where cruise ships berth. Just in front – should you already be hungry at this point – there's great dim sum at **Jade Garden**, see ⑪①.

Former Marine Police HQ

Just across Canton Road is a white stucco 19th-century building that was the Marine Police Headquarters until 1996. It has now been beautifully restored and reopened as **Hullett House** (www.hulletthouse.com), a 10-suite boutique hotel, with five restaurants. Below Hullett House, the small hill that gave marine policemen their vantage point has been converted into a brand-new faux-Victorian mall called 1881 Heritage.

The KCR Station Clock Tower

Head back to the harbour and the 45m (147ft) -tall brick-and-stone **clock tower** dating from 1915. This is all that remains of the grand Kowloon–Canton Railway Terminus, demolished in 1978.

From here you could once take a train all the way to Paris.

Take the staircase near the clock tower up to the elevated promenade and observation gallery. The waterfront here offers such magnificent vistas of Hong Kong Island that it's hard to figure out what inspired the architect to design a windowless façade for the **Hong Kong Cultural Centre ❷** (tel: 2734 2009; www.hkculturalcentre.gov. hk). What's more, it is covered in what appear to be cut-price bathroom tiles. But aesthetics aside, the building is Hong Kong's premier venue for classical Western and Chinese music, ballet and theatre. It is home base to the HK Philharmonic and HK Chinese orchestras, and attracts top performers from the international circuit as well as local musicians. Find the entrance opposite César's *Flying Frenchman* sculpture to check if there are any performances you'd like to see.

Above from far left:
at the opera; the bright lights of Tsim Sha Tsui.

Stylish Arrival
Arrive at TST in style on board *aqua luna*, a red-sail junk that offers eight daily 45-minute cruises around the harbour from Central Pier (tel: 2116 8821; www. aqualuna.com.hk).

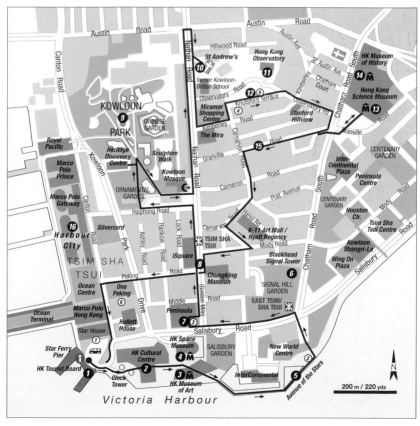

Hong Kong Museum of Art

Walk through the Cultural Centre to the **Hong Kong Museum of Art** ❸ (tel: 2721 0116; Fri and Sun–Wed 10am–6pm, Sat 10am–8pm; charge except Wed). It has superb collections of Chinese antiquities, paintings and calligraphy, contemporary Hong Kong art, and, perhaps most fascinating for many, pictures of old Hong Kong, Canton and Macau (third floor).

Hong Kong Space Museum

The large white dome just beyond it is the **Hong Kong Space Museum** ❹ (tel: 2721 0226; Mon and Wed–Fri 1–9pm, Sat–Sun 10am–9pm; charge except Wed), with lots of interactive exhibits aimed to keep kids enthralled and a high-tech planetarium with an Omnimax film theatre.

ALONG THE WATERFRONT

Just to the east, the waterfront promenade turns into the **Avenue of the**

Buyer Beware
There are bargains to be had in the electronics bazaars and other stores on Nathan Road, but if a price sounds too good to be true, it probably is. Choose shops displaying the Tourist Board's QTS (Quality Tourism Services) scheme sticker.

Stars ❺, a 440m (480 yard) -long tribute to the Hong Kong movie industry, with the harbour providing a perfect backdrop. Acting and directing achievements are commemorated Hollywood-style with brass stars and handprints in the pavement, and there's a statue of Hong Kong's most famous film star, Bruce Lee, and souvenir shops with Hong Kong movie memorabilia. For a lingering look at the harbour view, the terrace at **Blues by the Bay**, see ⑪②, makes a handy stop, or turn away from the harbour and walk through the New World Centre mall to Salisbury Road. The new East Tsim Sha Tsui KCR train station is right across the street. Overlooking the new transport link is **Blackhead Signal Tower** ❻ (daily 9–11am and 4–6pm; free). The tower was built in 1907 to house the time-ball by which ships in the harbour adjusted their chronometers. From here, turn westwards back through an underground mall to the Peninsula hotel.

The Peninsula

The **Peninsula** ❼ *(see p.114)* is the *grande dame* of Hong Kong hotels, and first choice for visiting celebrities and heads of state since it opened in 1928. Hong Kong's only historic hotel also keeps up with the times, having gained a 30-storey central tower (crowned with a helipad) in the 1990s, which has enabled it to add the spectacular restaurant-bar **Felix**, see ⑪③, to its superb gourmet French restaurant Gaddi's and other facilities. However, it is the beautifully restored Peninsula Lobby that

---

Food and Drink 🍴

② BLUES BY THE BAY
Shop L012B, G/F New World Centre, 18–24 Salisbury Road, Tsim Sha Tsui; tel: 2739 3366; $$
Outdoor tables on the TST waterfront allow you to take in a panorama of the harbour and the Hong Kong Island skyline. To eat there's a fashionable, international mix of cuisines with Thai leanings, accompanied most evenings by live music.

③ FELIX
28/F Peninsula Hotel, Salisbury Road, Tsim Sha Tsui; tel: 2315 3188; $$$$
A top-floor restaurant-bar that's not to be missed, with dazzling views, ultra-chic Philippe Starck decor and delectable Pacific Rim cuisine. Drop by just for a cocktail if nothing else, but dress smart, and feel like the proverbial million dollars.

wins most visitors' hearts – a wonderfully atmospheric place to stop for coffee or a full afternoon tea (daily 2–7pm). In recognition of its popularity, the dress code is a little more relaxed before 6.30pm.

THE GOLDEN MILE

Leave the hotel via the Peninsula Shopping Arcade to exit onto bustling **Nathan Road** ❽, a canyon of neon lined with hotels, restaurants and shops that's dubbed the 'Golden Mile' in the tourist brochures, though it stretches away for several miles at least. Delightfully bright and brash and with teeming streets and forests of colourful illuminated signs, this whole area of TST fits most people's preconceptions of Hong Kong.

Electronics shops abound on either side of this part of Nathan Road, and off to the west side of the main drag Peking, Hankow and Haiphong roads are also full of small shops and stores.

Kowloon Park
Halfway along Haiphong Road you will find the south entrance of **Kowloon Park** ❾ (daily 6am–midnight; free). Occupying the site of a former British military barracks, the park is a breath of fresh air for nearby residents and office workers, with lakes, ornamental gardens, aviaries, swimming pools and a sports complex.

The **Hong Kong Heritage Discovery Centre** (Fri–Wed 10am–6pm; free), which houses a permanent display on Hong Kong culture, occupies

two surviving blocks of the old 1910 Whitfield Barracks within the park. Art-lovers will enjoy the open-air **Sculpture Walk**, in the southeast corner. On Sunday afternoons there are demonstrations of Chinese martial arts here (tel: 2724 3344; Sun 2.30–4.30pm; free).

Leave the park by the entrance beside the imposing **Kowloon Mosque**, the largest one in Hong Kong, recognisable by its magnificent white marble dome and four minarets.

Above from far left: on the Star Ferry; Bruce Lee statue; Kowloon Park; neon-drenched Golden Mile of Nathan Road.

Hollywood East

With the opening of the 'Avenue of the Stars' in 2004 Hong Kong paid tribute to its home-grown film industry. This is the entertainment capital of East Asia, and Hong Kong films and music draw vast audiences from Singapore to Japan. From simple beginnings with crudely shot martial arts pictures in the 1960s, the industry has got ever more ambitious, and its products run from the inimitable acrobatics of Jackie Chan to lavish epics made with mainland China such as *Hero*. A feature of the scene is that its stars – typical of HK – are hyperactive, and work in many fields: Andy Lau, for example, hugely popular star of gangster dramas like *Infernal Affairs* – remade by Martin Scorsese as *The Departed* – is just as much a superstar of the Canto-pop music scene.

Above from left:
made-to-measure
suits; inviting
dim sum restaurant.

Below: typical flats
in Tsim Sha Tsui.

EAST OF NATHAN ROAD

Continue north along Nathan Road to cross over at the junction of Austin Road, then walk back a little way down the opposite side past the Victorian-Gothic-style building at no. 138, under aged banyan trees – **St Andrew's Church** ❿ (1904), the oldest Anglican church in Kowloon, Next door, at no. 136, set back from the road, is the former **Kowloon-British School**, from 1902. Further up the hill on Observatory Road is the **Hong Kong Observatory** ⓫, another fine colonial building, from 1883. Visits are by appointment only (tel: 2721 2326).

Knutsford Terrace

Carry on down Nathan Road and turn east into Kimberley Road: to your left, opposite the turning into Carnarvon Road, are **Knutsford Terrace** ⓬ and Knutsford Steps, a discreet stretch that is one of the most popular places in Kowloon for alfresco dining and socialising, and an ideal spot to break for lunch with a good choice of international restaurants, see ⓫④ and ⑤.

CHATHAM ROAD

After lunch, head east along Knutsford Terrace to join Observatory Road, passing the Stanford Hillview Hotel, and walk down to the junction with **Chatham Road South**. It's difficult to believe, but this junction marked the original waterfront prior to the huge reclamation that now forms Tsim Sha Tsui East. Turn right and cross over Chatham Road South by the raised pedestrian walkway at Granville Road.

Hong Kong Science Museum

Follow the signs to the **Hong Kong Science Museum** ⓭ (tel: 2732 3232; Mon–Wed and Fri 1–9pm; Sat–Sun 10am–9pm; charge except Wed), a wonderland of interactive exhibits aimed towards schoolchildren.

Hong Kong Museum of History

Next door is the **Hong Kong Museum of History** ⓮ (tel: 2724 9042; Mon and Wed–Sat 10am–6pm; Sun 10am–7pm;

charge except Wed). The collection traces every aspect of the remarkable evolution of Hong Kong, from its days as a peaceful rural backwater to colonial times and the teeming metropolis of today. The displays are well thought-out and executed with aplomb.

FACTORY SHOPS AND MEGAMALLS

Head back across Chatham Road and then west along **Granville Road ⓯**, well known for its 'factory-outlet' shops selling cheap 'seconds' – overruns of garments manufactured in mainland China for export. There's also a big mix of fashion boutiques and accessory shops here – as well as in the adjacent streets – that makes the area fascinating to explore, especially Cameron Road, Carnarvon Road and Mody Road. These streets on the east side of Nathan Road are also home to the greatest concentration of Hong Kong's famous Indian tailors, who produce suits and dresses in record time.

Back to the Harbourside
From Mody Road, cross over Nathan Road once again and head along Peking Road to Canton Road. Straight in front of you will be the gargantuan **Harbour City ⓰** complex, a maze of hotels and interconnecting malls that stretches almost the whole length of Canton Road.

To end the day, head back to the harbourside and ferry pier to enjoy the nightly fireworks at 8pm, or take the lift up to **Aqua**, see ⑪⑥, for some of HK's best bar-stools with a view.

Above: the mosque; dinosaur exhibit at the Science Museum.

Food and Drink 🍴

④ BLACK STUMP AUSTRALIAN GRILL & BAR
G/F 1 Knutsford Terrace, Tsim Sha Tsui; tel: 2721 0202; $$
Choose from seafood, salads and Italian dishes such as pasta. The set lunches offer particularly good value. Each table has its own beer pump.

⑤ HEAVEN AND EARTH
G/F and 1/F 6 Knutsford Terrace; tel: 2367 8428; $$–$$$
Colourful and kitsch Chinese eatery, featuring dishes inspired by Shanghai, Sichuan and Taiwan cuisine and delicious plates from all over China. It's an easy place to pop in for a bowl of noodles or a light meal rather than a full Chinese banquet. Head upstairs for dining.

⑥ AQUA
29–30/F One Peking, 1 Peking Road; Tsim Sha Tsui; tel: 3427 2288; $$$$
A knockout demonstration of Hong Kong style, this glamorous bar and restaurant has three separate areas on the top floors of One Peking, all with fabulous floor-to-ceiling views of Hong Kong Island and Kowloon. Aqua Roma and Aqua Tokyo offer a choice between superb Italian or Japanese food, while Aqua Spirit has to be one of the world's most stunning places to linger over a cocktail. Note that they have a minimum charge, however – HK$420 per person for dinner and HK$165 (the rough price of a cocktail) at Aqua Spirit, the restaurant's bar.

Urban Regeneration
After Kai Tak Airport closed, Kowloon's height limits were lifted. The second-tallest building for now is the 64-floor, 261m (856ft) K11 tower (2007), which includes the Hyatt Regency Hong Kong and the trendy K11 Art Mall, on Hanoi Road above an MTR exit.

YAU MA TEI AND MONG KOK

Experience the authentic Chinese flavour of Hong Kong and some of its most fascinating traditions – and pick up some bargains – on this walk through the buzzing markets at the heart of Kowloon.

DISTANCE 4.5km (2¾ miles)
TIME Half a day
START Jordan MTR
END Prince Edward MTR
POINTS TO NOTE

Potentially a long walk through the streets and markets either side of Nathan Road, but with plenty to distract you along the way, and possible stops. If time starts to run short, you're never far from the MTR.

Food and Drink

① **PEKING RESTAURANT**
1/F 227 Nathan Road, Jordan; tel: 2730 1315; $
While in the Jordan area track down this straightforward traditional restaurant for classic Northern Chinese dishes such as roast Peking duck with spring onions and pancakes.

② **LIGHT VEGETARIAN RESTAURANT**
G/F New Lucky House, 13 Jordan Road, Yau Ma Tei; tel: 2384 2833; $
Lots of dishes based on Cantonese favourites, but in vegetarian form – think noodles, imitation meat dishes – plus enjoyable stir-fries and even vegetarian dim sum. Excellent value for money.

③ **KUBRIK**
Broadway Cinémathèque, Prosperous Gardens, 3 Public Square Street, Yau Ma Tei; tel: 2384 8929; $
Packed with books on Western and Chinese film, plus movie-related gifts, Kubrik does cakes and coffees plus a short menu of international dishes for lunch and dinner.

TEMPLE STREET

Emerge from Exit C2 of Jordan MTR station onto Bowring Street, known for fabric shops and clothes stalls. Should you already be hungry, there's the old-style **Peking Restaurant** on the corner, and the **Light Vegetarian** not far away, see ① and ②.

Walk down Bowring, turn right up Woosung Street to busy Jordan Road, then head one block west and right up **Temple Street ❶**, famous for its **night market**. By day, the first few blocks are a centre for wholesale jewellery suppliers. If you're thirsty, stop at one of the open-fronted tea shops and try one of the herbal brews.

The Jade Market

Turn left at Saigon Street and continue along past the mix of small shops, *cha chan tengs* (a Hong Kong-style café or diner typically with formica tables and fluorescent lights serving quick cheap food) and roast-meat shops marked by glazed, flattened ducks hanging outside. Turn right up Reclamation Street, with its lively food market (not for the squeamish), to Kansu Street.

Beneath the highway bridge is the **Jade Market ❷** (daily 10am–4pm),

Above from far left:
Temple Street Market;
bangles at the Jade
Market; tea shop;
flower market.

packed with stalls hawking everything from top-grade jade to cheap glass trinkets. Genuine jade can range in colour from a milky white to deep translucent green; fault lines or specks lower the value, and the best stones are uniform in colour and cool to the touch. Jade has many imitations so, unless you have expert advice, it's probably best to focus less on potential value and stick instead to pieces you like for their decorative value. Be prepared to bargain.

If you need a break, head west across Public Square Street to the Broadway Cinémathèque arts cinema (Prosperous Gardens), which is also home to **Kubrik**, a cute café and film bookshop, see ⑪③.

TEMPLES AND FORTUNE TELLERS

By the small fruit-and-vegetable market on Kansu Street, turn left into Shanghai Street and walk north to the 120-year-old **Tin Hau Temple ❸** (daily 7am–5.30pm; free, donations appreciated). The fishermen's goddess Tin Hau is worshipped in the large temple by the main entrance, with spirals of incense falling from the ceiling, an ornate altar with gold effigies and fanciful lanterns. Other temples in the complex are dedicated to Shing Wong, Hong Kong's 'city god', Fook Tak, an earth god, and Guanyin, goddess of mercy. Fortune-tellers, some English-speaking, ply their ancient trade at the south end of the complex (*see feature p.71*), and old men play cards and chess in the park outside.

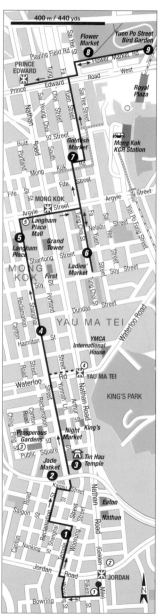

Late Shopping

Although it opens up earlier (around 2pm), the best time to visit Temple Street Night Market, as the name suggests, is in the evenings (6–10pm), when it fills with after-work crowds, looking to bargain for cheap clothes, DVDs and gadgets. You can also catch impromptu performances of Cantonese opera, and feast on the little *siu yei* sweet-and-sour snacks from *dai pai dong* food stalls.

Above: birds at market; a quick lunch.

CENTRAL YAU MA TEI

The next stretch of Shanghai Street is lined with shops selling altar shrines, statues of Buddhist and Daoist deities, and feng shui mirrors and compasses. There are also plenty of shops selling traditional kitchen implements, such as bamboo steamers, chopping boards and wooden biscuit-moulds. Further along Shanghai Street you will find a small park, where elderly men while away the hours by comparing their caged songbirds.

Sesame Streets

If your feet are tired, turn right at Waterloo Road to Yau Ma Tei MTR station. Stop off for a vegetarian snack, see ⑪④, or go straight away one stop north to Mong Kok MTR (Nelson Street exit). Otherwise, continue walking north along Shanghai Street as far as Argyle Street. This takes you through the heart of **Yau Ma Tei ❹** ('Place of Sesame Plants'). Although the waterfront has moved about a kilometre to the west, the connection with the sea is still evident in the seafood restaurants, wet-fish trade and traditional artisan workshops.

MONG KOK

Beyond Soy Street, you enter Mong Kok ('Busy Place') – one of the densest urban districts in the world, and once infamous for brothels and triad activity There's been a concerted effort to 'clean up' the area in recent years, and the 2004 opening of the **Langham Place ❺** complex at the corner of Shanghai and Argyle streets has transformed this part of Mong Kok, with a luxury hotel, office towers, a dazzling mall and a modern range of **restaurants**, including **The Place**, see ⑪⑤.

Nevertheless, the old grittiness and street theatre of everyday Kowloon life are not too hard to find. New interest in Hong Kong heritage means that efforts are now being made to preserve what's left: just across the Argyle Street junction from Langham Place, a group of pre-World War II colonnaded buildings, or 'shop houses', at 600–626 Shanghai Street are being conserved.

Mong Kok's Markets

To reach the **Ladies' Market** ❻ (daily noon–10.30pm), walk two blocks east along Argyle to **Tung Choi Street**, and turn right. Here you'll find hundreds of stalls selling cheap T-shirts, jeans, lingerie, gadgets and gimmicky souvenirs, plus women's accessories, which vaguely justify the market's name. Then retrace your steps to cross Argyle Street and Mong Kok Road to the part of Tung Choi Street known as the **Goldfish Market** ❼ (daily 10am–6pm), where Hong Kong people buy the fish and aquariums considered good for feng shui. The parallel section of **Fa Yuen Street** is lined with factory outlets, and is good for picking up fashion bargains.

Flowers and Songbirds

At the north end of Fa Yuen Street, cross busy Prince Edward Road West,

head one block east, take the first left into Sai Yee Street then right into fragrant Flower Market Road, home to Hong Kong's premier **Flower Market** ❽ (daily 10am–6pm). At the far end you'll find the **Yuen Po Street Bird Garden** ❾ (daily 10am–6pm), where thousands of songbirds are displayed in intricate bamboo or wooden cages (also for sale, and great souvenirs). The birds are valued not so much for their appearance as their singing abilities. Return to Prince Edward Road West and head west to reach Prince Edward MTR.

Above from far left:
Yuen Po Street
Bird Garden;
Goldfish Market.

Opposite below:
neon lights and late-night shopping.

Food and Drink 🍴

④ JOYFUL VEGETARIAN
530 Nathan Road, Yau Ma Tei;
tel: 2780 2230; $
Another of Kowloon's engaging, and surprising, set of vegetarian options: run by Buddhists, it offers an impressive variety, but the highlight is the delicious country-style hotpot.

⑤ THE PLACE
Langham Place Hotel, 555 Shanghai Street, Mong Kok; tel: 3552 3388; $$$$
The open kitchen adds excitement to this relaxed yet impressive restaurant in Mong Kok's top hotel. The menu is sophisticated and international – from fresh, light Mediterranean salads to pan-Asian specialities.

Know Your Fortune

The belief in fortune-telling is as old as China, and fortune-tellers can be found clustered around many of Hong Kong's temples – but above all the Tin Hau in Yau Ma Tei and Wong Tai Sin temple in north Kowloon, near the MTR station of the same name. You can have your destiny read in your palm, your face, or both; all around you, you'll also hear the rattling sound of *chim*. These are sticks of bamboo, each marked with a number and a phrase. You rattle several together in a special canister until one falls out, and then hand it to the fortune-teller for interpretation. Other, much more complex, consultations involve drawing up a whole life-chart for you on the basis of Chinese astrology, for which you may be asked to provide a real gamut of information.

LANTAU

This tour visits rugged, mountainous Lantau, Hong Kong's largest island. The Po Lin Monastery and its Big Buddha, the fishing village at Tai O and some fine beaches and majestic mountain scenery make it a popular retreat.

DISTANCE 21km (13 miles)
TIME A full day
START Mui Wo
END Tung Chung MTR
POINTS TO NOTE

Lantau's main sights can be covered in a day, but it's best to start early, and avoid Sundays and holidays. Ferries to the starting point, Mui Wo (Silvermine Bay), go from Central Ferry Pier no. 6.

Transport in Lantau

Green taxis or buses will take you round Lantau. If you want to take a cable car up to Ngong Ping and the Big Buddha, catch bus 3M to Tung Chung from Mui Wo, or take the MTR to Tung Chung.

PO LIN

At **Mui Wo ❶**, take a no. 2 bus to Ngong Ping. The 45-minute ride takes you past lovely coastal scenery, including **Cheung Sha ❷**, Hong Kong's longest beach, and into the mountains.

The Big Buddha

From the end of the bus route, walk up to the sprawling red, orange and gold **Po Lin Monastery ❸**, Hong Kong's

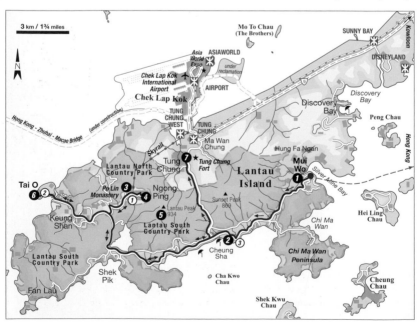

largest Buddhist shrine. Founded in 1905, Po Lin's temples and gardens are dominated by **Big Buddha**, at 24m (79ft) the world's largest outdoor bronze Buddha. The monastery's restaurant, see ⑪①, serves great vegetarian food.

Adding to Po Lin's popularity is **Ngong Ping Village ❹** (daily 10am–6pm; charges to some attractions), a newly built Chinese village, with shops, a traditional tea house and theatres showing Buddhist-themed tales. It is also the terminus for the **Ngong Ping 360 Skyrail cable car** (10am–6pm weekdays, 9.30am–6.30pm weekends), which runs to Tung Chung. On clear days, views on the 25-minute journey across Lantau are dramatic.

If you prefer to keep your feet firmly on the ground and are feeling energetic, you can follow the steep trail from here to **Lantau Peak ❺**, at 934m/3,064ft, Hong Kong's second-highest mountain. The views are glorious.

TAI O

Now take bus no. 21 to Tai O. The 20-minute journey passes several splendid monasteries, hidden high on wooded hillsides, before reaching **Tai O ❻**. A fishing village built on stilts, it was long cut off from most of Hong Kong by the mountains. Its distinctive metal-and-wood stilt houses were built over the creek by Tanka fishing people so that they could stay as close to the water as possible. However, overfishing has now led to a decline in the industry, and, ironically, most of the dried fish (once a local spe-ciality) sold on its narrow streets is imported from the Philippines.

Village Sights

In the centre of the village is the **Hau Wong Temple** (1699), the oldest of four temples in the Territory dedicated to the guardian of the Song Dynasty boy emperors during their time in exile in Hong Kong. Tai O is also home to the **Hong Kong Shaolin Wushu Centre** (www. shaolincc.hk), which has courses in the famous Shaolin techniques of Chinese martial arts. For a pit stop in the village, try the no-frills **Good View**, see ⑪②. Alternatively, take bus no. 11 to Tung Chung and head to the beach at Cheung Sha for **The Stoep**, see ⑪③.

TUNG CHUNG

From Tai O the no. 11 bus will take you to **Tung Chung ❼**, end of the MTR line from the city. Take a look at **Tung Chung Fort**, built for the Qing emperors in pre-British days.

Above from far left: beach near Lantau; Big Buddha; burning incense at Po Lin; dragon boat.

Ngong Ping 360 Skyrail
If you want to take in the views from the Skyrail cable care check www.np360. com.hk to make sure that it is running. Certain weather conditions and maintenance may affect the schedule.

Below: Po Lin.

Food and Drink

① PO LIN MONASTERY RESTAURANT
Ngong Ping, Lantau; tel: 2985 5248; $
The monastery's two huge, canteen-like dining rooms provide excellent vegetarian lunches from 11.30am–5pm.

② GOOD VIEW SEAFOOD RESTAURANT
15 Wing On Street, Tai O; tel: 2985 5115; $
There's actually not much of a view from this fluorescent-lit dining room. Cantonese-style seafood and staples. Fine for a quick bite.

③ THE STOEP
32 Lower Cheung Sha Village, Lantai; tel: 2980 2699; $$
Relaxed outdoor dining South African-style. Feast on home-made bread, *bobotie* (like meatloaf) and a *braii* (barbecue) on the beach.

HONG KONG DISNEYLAND

Opened in 2005, the world's fifth 'Magic Kingdom' is smaller than its older cousins in Tokyo, Paris and the US, but for families with kids trying to take in all the rides and shows in Hong Kong's summer heat and humidity, its manageable size might be just about right.

Beat the Crowds

Avoid visiting the park during the three major holiday periods on the Chinese mainland, each of them one week long – Chinese New Year, and the first weeks of May and October. These are also known as the 'Golden Weeks'.

Below: transport, Disney-style.

DISTANCE N/A – tour is based in one place
TIME A full day
START/END Disneyland
POINTS TO NOTE

The resort is a 25-minute ride from Central on the MTR Tung Chung line. Change at Sunny Bay onto the special train to Disneyland Resort Station. For full details and admission prices, see www.hongkongdisneyland.com or call tel: 1830 830. All year there are many special promotions, and late opening at Chinese New Year and Halloween. Overnight Stay: to immerse yourself in the Disney experience stay at the Hong Kong Disneyland Hotel (from HK$1,800) or Hollywood Hotel (from HK$1,300): check the website for special offers for resort hotels' guests.

Veterans of Disneyland parks will find most things familiar to them at the Hong Kong version. From the Victorian-style **Disneyland Resort Station** it's a five-minute walk to the entrance. Inside, you'll find yourself in **Main Street USA ❶**, the first of the four themed 'lands'. Pick up a map at **City Hall**, and walk through Disney's ideal version of small-town America in the early 1900s. Old-fashioned vehicles and Disney characters populate the streets, and this area has the biggest concentration of shops and restaurants. At the **Opera House** you can see the story of Disneyland, and at the **Animation Academy** you can see how cartoons are created. Catch the **Disneyland Railroad** to move on to the other lands.

The park does have its special features. It's smaller than the other Disneylands, but it is expanding. The most visible difference is in the catering: in recognition of the central role of a proper meal in the Chinese idea of a family day out, there are proportionately more food outlets, and most offer a wide choice of Chinese and Asian cuisines, such as Main Street's **Plaza Inn**, see ⑪①, although American and international options can naturally be had as well. Another, much-trumpeted peculiarity is that Disney employed a

squad of feng shui and Chinese numerology experts in designing the park. Among their contributions are: it has its back to a mountain, and faces the sea; it has many water features, beneficial in feng shui; it has more red (considered a lucky colour) in the design than usual; and there are no green hats for sale, since in China a man in a green hat is said to be untrustworthy.

FANTASYLAND

Step through the gates of Sleeping Beauty Castle into **Fantasyland ❷**, where characters from *Snow White* or the *Aristocats* wander around rides such as Cinderella's Carousel and Dumbo's Flying Elephants. For respite from the heat, take in the *Golden Mickeys* show, then have a spin on the Mad Hatter's Tea Cups. The plaza in front of the castle is a good spot for watching the nightly **fireworks**. Fantasyland also has the park's grandest restaurant in the **Royal Banquet Hall**, see ⑪②.

TOMORROWLAND

With the focus on space and exploration, the rides in **Tomorrowland ❸** are the biggest hits with older kids: Space Mountain, Orbitron, Buzz Lightyear Astro Blasters, the wild Autopia car ride and more.

ADVENTURELAND

Jungle journeys and mysterious creatures are the order of the day in **Adventureland ❹**. Get a Fastpass *(see right)* for the Festival of the Lion King Show, a 30-minute musical that runs several times daily, and take a cruise to Tarzan's Treehouse – but watch out for the Liki Tiki talking totems.

Above from far left: Sleeping Beauty Castle; Minnie Mouse and friend.

Fastpass

Queues can be long at the most popular rides and shows – up to 40 minutes – and the best way to avoid them is with the Fastpass system. When you arrive at the park, insert your admission ticket in a Fastpass Machine at each attraction, and for no extra charge you can book a Fastpass ticket for a specific time. When your time comes around, go straight onto the ride, without joining the queue.

Food and Drink 🍴

① PLAZA INN
Main Street USA; $$
There are Plaza restaurants at all the Disneyland parks: this one looks the same from outside, but go in and you'll find classic Cantonese dishes, including dim sum, served the old-fashioned way from trolleys.

② ROYAL BANQUET HALL
Fantasyland; $$–$$$
The resort's smartest eatery follows an Asian concept of 'four kitchens': the kettle kitchen offers curries and stews; the steam kitchen dumplings and dim sum; the grill kitchen barbecued fish and meats; and the last Japanese tempura and sushi.

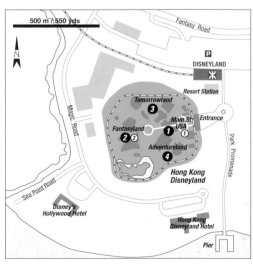

14

LAMMA

Leave the metropolis behind and take a leisurely hike across the hills and beaches of car-free, slow-paced Lamma Island, followed by a seafood lunch by the harbour in the little village of Sok Kwu Wan.

Above: local calligrapher; there are no cars on Lamma, so either walk or hire a bike to get around.

DISTANCE 6km (4 miles)
TIME A full day
START/END Outlying Islands Ferry Piers
POINTS TO NOTE

Ferries run from Central Ferry Pier no. 4 to two points on Lamma, Yung Shue Wan (every 30–60 mins), and, less frequently, to Sok Kwu Wan. The journey takes around 30 mins. There is a well-marked, paved path across the island between the two villages. Check the ferry schedule before you start dinner, as ferries back from Sok Kwu Wan can be two hours apart.

Food and Drink

① SAMPAN SEAFOOD RESTAURANT

16 Main Street, Yung Shue Wan; tel: 2982 2388; $
Open from 7am daily, the Sampan serves alfresco dim sum until around 11am; simply go up to the counter, check out the baskets and order what takes your fancy. For lunch and dinner, there's a full Cantonese menu. Enjoy harbour views and taking in village life while feasting. Huge tanks of live fish and crustaceans both entertain and sustain diners.

② BOOKWORM CAFÉ

79 Main Street, Yung Shue Wan; tel: 2982 4838; $–$$
Consistently good vegetarian and vegan food. Choose from a long menu of vegetarian staples, salads, juices and home-made cakes: shepherdess pie and veggie burgers are among the more filling choices. Situated close to the Tin Hau Temple.

Lamma's rolling hills, bays, beaches, easy-going seafood restaurants and tiny villages of three-storey houses are quite a contrast to high-rise Hong Kong. A few Hong Kong city-dwellers who visit Lamma like it so much they stay: for some a half-hour commute to Central on a ferry is a small price to pay for a greener, car-free environment where rents are lower.

The island's population hovers at around 6,000, including a disproportionate number of expatriates, from over 60 countries at the last count. There's a different pace of life here, and walking or biking are the only way to get about for residents and visitors alike. You can hire bikes for a very reasonable price at the Hoi Nam Bicycle Shop in Sha Po Village, close to the Main Street.

Apart from Lamma's many dogs, the only thing you have to beware of on the island's paths are the small motorised trucks used for delivering heavy goods and its toytown-sized ambulances and fire engines.

YUNG SHUE WAN

From the pier in **Yung Shue Wan ❶**, walk down the bicycle-lined jetty and take a look at the map of the island to get your bearings. Lamma is well sign-

posted, and if you stick to the main pathways it is difficult to get lost. Yung Shue Wan, in the northwest, is the main village. All activity centres around the Main Street that follows the sweep of the bay, where you will find the post office, open-air seafood restaurants, pubs, grocery shops, gift shops and cafés serving Chinese, Western, Japanese and Indian food.

Stop for a dim sum breakfast at the **Sampan Seafood Restaurant**, see ①①, or carry on to the end of Main Street and the New Age stalwart the vegetarian **Bookworm Café**, see ①②.

The Tin Hau Temple

Walk for about another minute and you will find the village's well-tended **Tin Hau Temple**, next to the football pitch. Until the 1970s the fishing com-

munities of Lamma were fairly isolated, and traditions associated with the sea were central parts of local life. Yung Shue Wan celebrates the birthday of the fishermen's protector Tin Hau each May with a dragon boat race in the harbour, lion dances and ceremonies at the temple and a week of Cantonese opera in a temporary bamboo opera house, which is built on the football pitch.

Retrace your steps back to Main Street, turn right onto Back Street and head south out of the village past shops and Thai, Turkish, Italian and Chinese restaurants, following the signs for Hung Shing Ye beach. Walk through a series of increasingly small villages that give way to greenery, all the while keeping Lamma's landmark power station *(see feature p.79)* on your right.

(see feature p.79)

Above from far left: temple offerings at the Tin Hau Temple; dragon boat in action.

Below left: junk sailing near Lamma.

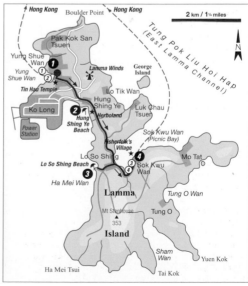

Food and Drink

③ RAINBOW SEAFOOD RESTAURANT

16–20 First Street, Sok Kwu Wan; tel: 2982 8100; $$

A local institution, the giant Rainbow is by far the largest of Sok Kwu Wan's restaurants. It's bustling and very enjoyable, with specialities such as garlic prawns and lobster in ten kinds of butter and very reasonable set menus.

④ PEACH GARDEN SEAFOOD RESTAURANT

8 First Street, Sok Kwu Wan; tel: 2982 8581; $–$$

Friendly family-run restaurant five minutes' walk beyond the big First Street venues. It has outdoor tables, tasty Cantonese cuisine and crab, prawns, etc, cooked to order.

BEACHES

Hung Shing Ye ❷ is a sandy well-managed beach manned by lifeguards. Pause for a paddle or a cup of herbal tea at **Herboland**, a small organic farm on the far side of the beach. After the farm the path climbs and dips steeply through the grassy hills, above rugged cliffs and small sandy bays. A pagoda and viewing platform mark the halfway point of the walk, and a map lets you see see how far you've come.

The path descends into a wooded valley at **Lo So Shing**. Bear right through the sleepy hamlet of traditional Chinese houses and right again at the sign to **Lo So Shing Beach ❸**. Fringed by woodland, this pretty beach, with lifeguards and showers, never gets too crowded on hot summer weekends, and is often deserted.

SOK KWU WAN

Rejoin the main path and turn right towards Sok Kwu Wan. Follow the path along the western rim of the bay with its floating fish farms, passing a former quarry that is now partly landscaped. The bay is overlooked by **Mount Stenhouse** (Shan Tei Tong) to the south, at 353m (1,160ft) Lamma's highest point. **Sok Kwu Wan ❹** village is home to only a few hundred people, and is dominated by the many seafood restaurants along the waterfront that are kept busy serving tour groups and junk trips.

All the restaurants are pretty good, and relaxing with a plate of seafood

and a cool drink overlooking the harbour is a favourite escape for Hong Kong residents. The **Rainbow**, see ⑪③, is the largest and best known, and has a website (www.rainbowrest.com.hk) and a free boat shuttle from the Central Ferry Piers (Pier 9) in Hong Kong. More low-key is the **Peach Garden**, see ⑪④, a five-minute walk along the main strip. You may spot a few celebrity photographs on display in Lamma's restaurants, including the island's most famous son, film star Chow Yun Fat.

Village Fisheries

To learn more about Lamma's indigenous population and fishing traditions visit the simple 'floating exhibition', situated amid the fish farms in the middle of the harbour, where fish are reared in underwater cages suspended from rafts. The entrance fee of around HK$40 (HK$30 for children) includes a short sampan ride out to the **Lamma Fisherfolk's Village**.

To return home, catch the Sok Kwu Wan ferry back to Central, or hike back to Yung Shue Wan.

Above from far left: dried fish is a speciality of the area; sea view. **Opposite below:** farmer sowing crops on Lamma.

Lamma Power

One easy way of identifying Lamma from a distance is by the three chimney stacks of Hong Kong Electric's power station, close to the island's most populated northwest tip. This coal-burning power station provides all the electricity for Hong Kong Island. In a recent nod to environmental concerns, Hong Kong Electric has built one 46m (151ft) wind turbine on the hillside facing Hong Kong Island. The company says it is using the project to gain experience in wind power, and the turbine saves 320 tonnes of coal a year; locals joke that the electricity it generates powers the displays at the exhibition centre at the foot of the windmill. Given its breezy open location, Lamma Winds – as it is officially called – is a pleasant spot to stroll up to and take in the views of huge container ships and tiny sampans on the Lamma Channel, especially if you haven't the time or energy to hike across the island. From the south end of Main Street in Yung Shue Wan, walk for five minutes until you reach a crossing with a wider 'road'. Turn left and follow this uphill for 15 minutes.

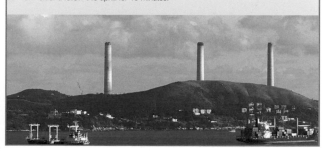

Ordering Fish
Fresh seafood is charged at that day's market price, so be sure to confirm the exact price and quantity when you order. Favourites include deep-fried squid, broccoli with scallops, minced quail and steamed garlic or piquant peppered prawns.

WESTERN NEW TERRITORIES

Well removed from the tourist trail, the New Territories stretch from the Kowloon hills to the mainland Chinese border. Within this sizeable area are high-rise new towns, temples and ancient walled villages, a wetland conservation park and Hong Kong's highest mountain.

The Hakka

The Hakka people came originally from North China, but were encouraged to migrate south by Chinese emperors, who expected them to be more loyal than native southerners. They long lived apart from their Cantonese-speaking neighbours, with their own dress (woman's hat shown above) and language. Today, most Hakka are integrated into Hong Kong life, but a few traditional Hakka villages remain.

DISTANCE Varies depending on route taken – see map opposite
TIME A full day
START/END Tsuen Wan MTR
POINTS TO NOTE
The New Territories can be explored easily by train and bus – and inexpensively, with an Octopus card *(see p.104)*. The MTR runs to Tsuen Wan, the KCR West railway line runs from the city to Tuen Mun, and the separate KCR Light Rail system goes around the northwestern towns. This area offers plenty of contrasts, so choose the places that appeal the most, and start early.

Almost 3.5 million people, around half Hong Kong's population, live in the New Territories, which have been absorbing Hong Kong's growing numbers since the 1970s. Although the new towns spread around the Territories such as Tsuen Wan, Tuen Mun, Yuen Long, Tai Po and Sha Tin have become huge population centres, much of the New Territories still consists of green hillsides – many now part of country parks – overlooking quiet villages.

HAKKA HERITAGE

The MTR line ends at **Tseun Wan ❶**. Follow the signs from Exit E to the **Sam Tung Uk Museum** (tel: 2411 2001; Wed–Mon 9am–5pm; free) on Kwu Uk Lane. In striking contrast to the modern housing estates that now surround it, this is a Hakka walled village, founded by the Chan clan in 1786. No longer inhabited, it was restored in the 1980s as a gem of a museum, displaying period Hakka furniture and farming implements, and hosting regular temporary exhibits on different aspects of the region's folk culture.

Along the Coast Road

Now head back to the MTR, and walk through it via Exit A2 to the bus terminus beneath the Nan Fung Centre. Catch a no. 66M bus to Tuen Mun

> ### Food and Drink 🍴
> **① MIU FAT MONASTERY**
> 18 Castle Peak Road, Lam Tei; tel: 2461 8567; $
> The second floor of the monastery houses a popular big canteen, serving enjoyable all-vegetarian lunches. Open noon–5pm only.

(journey time: 30–40 minutes). From the front seat on the top deck there are great views of the coast and the Tsing Kau and **Tsing Ma Bridges** as the bus winds along Tuen Mun Road.

In **Tuen Mun** ❷, get off at the Tai Hing Estate terminus, turn right along Tai Fong Street and left onto Tsun Wen Road. You can see the roof of your next destination, the Daoist **Ching Chung Koon Monastery** ❸ ahead, just beyond the highway bridge. The beautifully peaceful temple serves as a home for the elderly with no other means of support. It is also a repository for many Chinese art treasures, including lanterns that are more than 200 years old. The monastery is dedicated to Lui Tung Bun, one of the Eight Immortals, and contains lovely pavilions, lotus ponds and bonsai trees.

MIU FAT MONASTERY

Return to the Tai Hing Estate bus stop, and right in front is the Tai Hing South Light Rail (LRT) station. Take the 610 train for five stops to **Lam Tei**. Cross the tracks, and turn left at the main highway. **Miu Fat Buddhist Monastery** ❹ is on the other side of the road. On the top floor of this imposing three-storey building are three huge Buddhas, and there are plenty more statues all around the complex. It also has a very pleasant vegetarian **restaurant** for lunch, see ⑪①.

WETLAND PARK

From Lam Tei LRT station, take a no. 751 train, and change at Tin Tsz onto a 705 train to **Wetland Park** station.

Above from far left: golden Buddhas; veteran door guardian at a walled village, Kam Tin.

Birdwatching
It's also possible to explore a much more remote area of wetlands at Mai Po, east of the Wetlands Park. The Worldwide Fund for Nature (tel: 2526 4473, www.wwf.org.hk) runs regular tours.

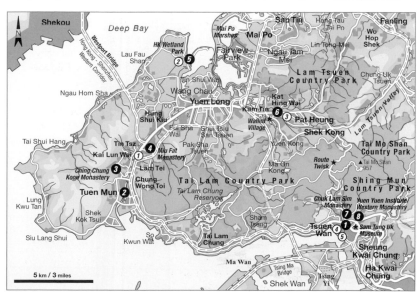

The Twisk Road
Route Twisk, the winding road that climbs up the flank of Tai Mo Shan between Tsuen Wan and Shek Kong, was carved across the New Territories by British army engineers in the 1950s, and was originally for military use only. It was first designated army-style as Route TW/SK – Tsuen Wan to Shek Kong – but a misprint in the project documents gave the road its strange label.

Above: decorative detail; shrine by the wayside.

The **Hong Kong Wetland Park 5** (tel: 2708 8885; www.wetlandpark. com; Wed–Mon 10am–5pm; charge) covers 61ha (151 acres), and introduces visitors to the diversity of Hong Kong's marshes. Sandwiched between the high rises of Tin Shui Wai and the mainland city of Shenzhen, the wetlands can be

explored on wooden boardwalks that meander through the park. There are some hides with telescopes for bird-watching, and so far 129 bird species have been recorded, including egrets, herons and the rare black-faced spoonbill. A large visitor centre houses a range of interactive exhibitions on the park and conservation. Should you get hungry, there's **Café de Coral**, see 🍴②, in the visitor centre.

WALLED VILLAGES

From Wetland Park station, take the 706 LRT train to **Tin Shui Wai**, and change to the KCR West rail line. Go three stops east to **Kam Sheung Road** station in **Kam Tin**. Leave through Exit B, cross the bridge and follow the footpath to the main road. **Kat Hing Wai 6** is on the next, parallel, road, but finding the connecting paths requires a little walking back and forth.

This is the most accessible of a set of walled villages around Kam Tin, which trace their roots back to the 12th century. It was the stronghold of the Tangs, one of the 'Five Great Clans' who dominated the area, a Cantonese clan who moved here from further north around 1150, and built most of Kat Hing Wai in the 1600s. Many of its inhabitants are still called Tang, although several Hakka now live here too. The walled compound has just one entrance, and one narrow main street; inside, many buildings have been modernised, but the way of life is still pretty traditional, and it's worth paying the HK$1 donation to enter. To take a

photo of the pipe-smoking Hakka women in their fringed hats, negotiate a small fee beforehand.

Kam Tin's nearby Indian-Nepalese **Shahjahan Restaurant**, see ⑪③, may seem out of place, but it opened when the British Army's Nepalese Gurkha regiments were based at Shek Kong Airfield. Today the Chinese PLA use the airfield, but unlike the Gurkhas and the British they do not leave the base.

MONASTIC GETAWAYS

From Kam Tin, the West Rail line will take you back to Kowloon; to continue the tour, though, head back to **Tsuen Wan** for more monasteries. Once there, walk inland up Tai Ho road to the MTR station. Just south of the station (Exit B) on Shui Wo Street are several bus stops, from where you can get a green minibus no. 85 to **Chuk Lam Sim Monastery ❼**. Tell the driver where you want to go, or just get off when you see the Thai-style shrine at the front of the monastery on the left. It has a lovely hillside location, and the main hall houses three golden Buddhas, around which are hundreds of Bodhisattva statues.

Three Temples in One

Alternatively, for a taste of all three major Chinese religions, visit the **Yuen Yuen Institute ❽** and the adjacent **Western Monastery**, both offering a pleasant escape from the city below. The Yuen Yuen is the only temple in Hong Kong devoted simultaneously to Daoism, Buddhism and Confucianism. The main hall is a scaled-down replica of the Temple of Heaven in Beijing, while the monastery has an eight-storey pagoda. Both are surrounded by halls, pavilions and gardens. To get there, take minibus no. 81 from Shui Wo Street to the last stop.

Eating in Tsuen Wan

If you are hungry in Tsuen Wan, most restaurants are located in or around two big malls just by the MTR station: conveyor-belt Japanese is served at **G-Sushi**, see ⑪④, in the **Nan Fung centre**, or cross the footbridge to Grand City Plaza and **Olive**, see ⑪⑤.

HK's Highest Peak

One of Hong Kong's wildest, most panoramic roads, the British Army's 'Route Twisk' *(see opposite)* twists and turns in spectacular fashion around its tallest peak, Tai Mo Shan, the 'big misty mountain', which at 957m (3,139ft) dwarfs the 552m (1,811ft) of Victoria Peak. To explore it, take the no. 51 bus between Kam Tin and Tsuen Wan, get off at the crossing with Tai Mo Shan Road and walk up to the Tai Mo Shan Country Park Visitor Centre. There are many good, well-indicated walks around the mountain, and in around 30 minutes you should be able to get near to the top, and enjoy superb vistas taking in both the mainland and Hong Kong Island.

SHENZHEN

Low-price shopping on a giant scale is the big draw of a trip to Hong Kong's gritty young neighbour, but this rapidly emerging city also claims the world's biggest golf centre and a cluster of popular theme parks.

Two Tips

- Shenzhen shops nearly always accept Hong Kong dollars, but you will pay less if you use Chinese *renminbi* (RMB), so change at least some of your cash at the border.
- Pickpocketing is more common in Shenzhen than Hong Kong, so take care of your valuables. Dress down, and do not wear expensive jewellery.

DISTANCE Varies
TIME A full day
START AND END Any East Rail MTR Station, Kowloon
POINTS TO NOTE

A passport with China visa is required for entry, and it is best to obtain your visa in advance (see p.107). Catch an MTR train to Lo Wu, from Kowloon Tong or any East Rail MTR station. Trains run every three minutes. At Lo Wu, get off and walk across the border into Shenzhen. Taxis are cheap and convenient, but make sure you have destinations written in Chinese and some small RMB notes.

By far the most successful of China's Special Economic Zones (SEZs), in two decades Shenzhen has grown into a rumbustious metropolis and one of the richest cities in China. Hong Kongers make regular trips across the border here for inexpensive recreation and bargains at its giant shopping bazaars.

Haggling is the order of the day at most Shenzhen shops – apart from in tailors' shops, where prices are more out in the open – and the cardinal rule is to bargain hard. Offer less than a third of the asking price, and settle for no more than half. Be prepared to walk away to see if the price will drop.

SHOPPING CENTRAL

Most visitors head to Shenzhen to shop, and many get no further than **Lo Wu Commercial City** ❶. It's impossible to miss: cross the border at Lo Wu, and as you leave the immigration building, the Shangri-La Hotel is in front, the railway station and tourist office are to the left, and on the right is the Lo Wu. With around 1,500 shops packed into five floors, it's easy to spend a whole day here. Soft furnishings, handbags, jewellery, electronics, fabrics, tailoring, oil paintings, ready-made 'designer' clothes and a cornucopia of other merchandise are all on sale. Shops selling the

Food and Drink

① TASTE
Shop 3008, Lo Wu Commercial City; tel: (0755) 8232 1773; $
With picture windows overlooking Shenzhen city, Taste – a meeting point – serves a mix of basic Western and Chinese food, Does Australian wine by the glass and surprisingly good coffee.

② LAUREL
Shop 5010, 5/F Lo Wu Commercial City; tel: (0755) 8232 3668; $$
A Shenzhen bargain, this popular restaurant offers inexpensive Cantonese food. Dim sum is served till 3pm. Expect to queue.

③ 360°
31/F Shangri-La Hotel, 1002 Jianshe Lu; tel: (0755) 8396 1380; $$$
Glitzy revolving restaurant on top of Shenzhen's landmark hotel, with an eclectic food menu.

same kind of items tend to be clustered together, while restaurants and massage centres (more spartan than spa-style) are grouped around the outside walls.

Baubles, Bangles and Tailoring

On the second and third floors you will find both costume jewellery and stall-holders selling precious and semi-precious stones, pearls and beads. Many will create new pieces to order.

Scores of tailors are located on the fifth floor. Many speak English or have someone to help with foreign clients: take a garment or just a picture of something you want copied, and then after a brief conversation your tailor will take you over to the fabric market, conveniently on the same floor, to choose your material. Some tailors will make up garments the same day, but if you are having suits or a few items made it's best to factor in a fitting and adjustments and then stay overnight.

Simple skirts and shirts can be as little as HK$80; suits and more complicated styles naturally cost more. Custom-made curtains and bed linen are also good value at Lo Wu – if you have all your home's measurements handy.

Essential Maintenance

After all this hectic buying and hag-gling, rest and relaxation are needed, and the Lo Wu can supply this too, in scores of small massage salons offering no-frills manicures and pedicures for men and women for approximately HK$20–40. There are also numerous places offering foot massages or other traditional Chinese treatments.

This huge mall also, of course, has places to eat, such as **Taste** and **Laurel**, see ⑪① and ⑪②. If the Lo Wu starts to feel claustrophobic, see another side of modern China by walking across the square to the **Shangri-La Hotel** and its top-floor **360°** bar-restaurant, see ⑪③.

Above from far left: vast Shenzhen shopping mall; the serious business of clothes shopping.

Shopping Etiquette
Do not follow anyone to an outlet or warehouse outside the centre – always stay in busy public places. If the item you want is off site, you can always wait at the shop while they collect it for you, or else ask if they can bring it to you at a central nail salon or restaurant.

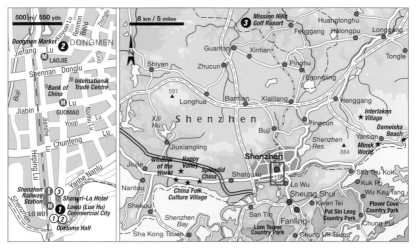

Above from left:
racks of suits; reminiscent of Lisbon: the wavy-patterned pavings in Macau's Largo de Senado.

BEYOND LO WU

Past the border-side shopping zone, the fascination of central Shenzhen is just in the city itself, given that 25 years ago it scarcely existed. A walk of about 1km (²/₃ mile) along Jianshe Lu, the main avenue, leads to **Dongmen** ❷, another shopping area packed with tailors. After dark, Shenzhen is home to a frenetic nightlife scene, spread across town.

There's still plenty more to do around here, but note it's advisable to use taxis to head beyond the centre. What seems like leisure facilities for the whole of southern China are stacked together here, notably **theme parks** *(see below)*.

Golfing Craze

Another thing people come here to do is play **golf**. China's new middle classes have taken to the game, and Hong Kongers play here because it's more affordable than closer to home. There are 12 full-size courses around Shenzhen, plus the world's largest golf resort at **Mission Hills** ❸ (www.missionhillsgroup.com), northeast of the city, with another 12 world-class courses just to itself, a luxury hotel and more. Courses offer packages, and will pick up golfers in Hong Kong.

Theme Parks

At times it's easy to see Shenzhen as one great big, peculiar theme park, but there's no shortage of the 'real thing'. There are no fewer than six fantasy-fun worlds within a 30km (18-mile) radius. Four are clustered together in the oddly named 'Overseas Chinese Town' (OCT), 15km (9 miles) west towards the port of Shekou. Window of the World (daily 9am–10.30pm; charge) showcases facsimiles of everything from Thai palaces and Japanese teahouses to the Sphinx and the Eiffel Tower; in a similar vein, Splendid China (daily 9am–9.30pm; charge) packs the whole country into one park; China Folk Culture Village (daily 9am–9.30pm; charge) presents 56 different ethnic perspectives; and Happy Valley (daily 9.30am–9pm; charge) keeps everyone happy with rides and water slides. To help you see them all, the Happy Line monorail links all four parks. Stranger still is Minsk World (daily 9am–7.30pm; charge), 12km (7 miles) east of Shenzhen, a 40,000-tonne former Soviet aircraft carrier. The OCT organisation is also expanding east of the city, near Shenzhen's beach resort of Dameisha, with Interlaken Village, a vast new park bizarrely imitating a Swiss mountain resort, with a luxury 'alpine hotel' (www.interlakenocthotel.com), golf courses, an ornamental tea plantation and the world's largest man-made waterfall.

MACAU: CITY TOUR

An hour from Hong Kong across the Pearl River, this tiny former Portuguese colony is packed with history and culinary traditions — plus gigantic casinos that ensure its role as the gambling capital of Asia.

In 1557 Portugal established the first European colony on Chinese soil in Macau, almost 300 years before the British claimed Hong Kong. The next 150 years went by fairly quietly, but things have changed quickly since Lisbon returned Macau to China in December 1999. Then Macau, like Hong Kong, became a Special Administrative Region (SAR) of the People's Republic of China — and its gaming industry was transformed.

Orientation

Macau is divided into the urban area on the peninsula linked to the Chinese mainland, and the former islands of **Taipa** and **Coloane**. Even the SAR's shape has been transformed by the gaming boom: these islands are now joined together by 620ha (1,500 acres) of reclaimed land, called the **Cotai Strip**, which has a key role in Macau's plan to become Asia's Las Vegas.

Some of 'old Macau' has survived, and has been preserved and restored in recent years. Several buildings grouped as the 'Historic Centre of Macau' were added to Unesco's World Heritage list in 2005, acknowledging the enclave's importance as the first example of European architecture on Chinese soil, and one of the first places where Eastern and Western cultures met.

DISTANCE 25km (15 miles)
TIME A full day
START Largo do Senado
END Centro Cultural de Macau
POINTS TO NOTE

Fast ferries run pretty much round the clock to Macau, and journey time is about one hour. Turbojet catamarans and hydrofoils (www.turbojet.com.hk) depart from the Macau Ferry Terminal at the Shun Tak Centre in Sheung Wan. New World First Ferry catamarans (www.nwff.com.hk) depart from China Ferry Terminal in Tsim Sha Tsui. The CoTai Jet (www.cotaijet.com.mo) runs from both Hong Kong terminals to the Taipa ferry terminal, which is closer to the airport and the Cotai Strip. Passports are required, but not a visa. Book ferry tickets in advance at weekends or holidays. Taxis aren't always easy to find in Macau, but the old centre is compact and good for walking.

Grand Prix

The Macau Grand Prix race is the biggest sporting event in Macau. The race starts and finishes at the Grand Prix Stand opposite the Macau Ferry Terminal, winding its way through 6km (4 miles) of city streets in between. The two-day event takes place on the third weekend in November, so book hotels or restaurants well ahead if you want to visit at that time.

LARGO DO SENADO

Catch a taxi or bus from the ferry pier — or just walk, for about 1.5km (1 mile) along Avenida da Amizade — to the centre of historic Macau, **Largo do Senado ❶**, the old city main square, paved with Portuguese mosaic cobblestones. The 'Historic Centre' buildings

Macau Basics

• Macau has its own currency, the *pataca* (indicated by MOP$), which is worth slightly less than the Hong Kong dollar, at around HK$1 = MOP$1.04. In practice, though, HK dollars are accepted everywhere in Macau, at a rate of one for one.

• To telephone Macau from Hong Kong, the code is 853.

are signposted with green and gold signs, and good maps are also available from the **tourist information centre** on the square (daily 9am–6pm). On the south side of the square is one of the finest creations of Portuguese colonial architecture in Macau, the **Leal Senado**, built in the 1780s and still the seat of Macau's municipal council.

It's easy to spend hours exploring the *travessões* (side streets), shops, markets, cafés and old buildings on and around Largo do Senado. The gracious white building on the east side of the square is the **Santa Casa da Misericórdia ②** (Holy House of Mercy; Mon–Sat 10am–1pm, 2.30–5.30pm; charge), established as a charitable mission in 1569, and now a museum. On the north

side of the square is the fine church of **São Domingos ③**. A chapel was begun here in 1597, and the yellow-walled Baroque church was com-pleted early in the next century. At the back of the church is the **Museum of Sacred Art** (daily 10am–6pm; free), with relics of the centuries of Catholic presence in Macau and south China.

Cafés and restaurants abound around Largo do Senado, so stop off to enjoy a coffee and Italian-style sandwich at **Caffè Toscana**, go for noodles at **Wong Chi Kei** or settle down for a French lunch at **Bonne Heure**, see ⓧ①–③.

São Paolo and the Fortaleza

From São Domingos walk north uphill to the ramp of steps beneath the **ruins**

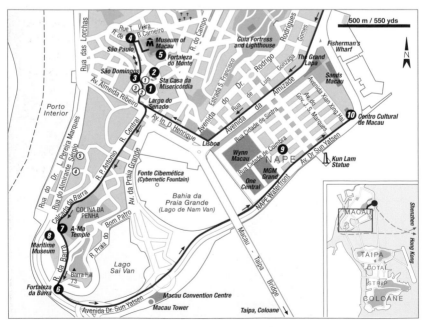

of São Paulo **❹**, Macau's most iconic monument. It was built from 1582 to 1638 as a giant church and Jesuit college, which trained missionaries who were sent all over Asia. Most of São Paulo burnt down in 1835, leaving only the façade, but this by itself is extraordinary, much of it elaborately carved by Japanese Christian exiles

Overlooking São Paulo is the **Fortaleza do Monte ❺** (daily 7am–7pm; free), often called Monte Fort. The structure dates from the early 1600s and still retains its impressive walls and cannons. The **Museum of Macau** (Tue–Sun 10am–6pm; charge), housed within the fortress, has well-captioned exhibits that chart the history of the colony and its people.

Food and Drink 🍴

① CAFFÈ TOSCANA
11 Travessa de São Domingos, Macau; tel: 2837 0354; $ $$
Likeable little Italian café with a mezzanine dining area, and good antipasti, pizza and fresh focaccia.

② WONG CHI KEI CONGEE & NOODLE
17 Largo do Senado, Macau; tel: 2833 1313; $
A bargain traditional-style Chinese restaurant handily situated on the main square. It opens late and does delicious bowls of wonton noodles.

③ LA BONNE HEURE
12A–B Travessa de São Domingos, Macau; tel: 2833 1209; $$
Authentic French cuisine prepared by a chef who trained under Joël Robuchon. It hosts regular art exhibitions, and stays open for drinks and music until 1am on Friday.

BARRA

Retrace your steps back to Largo do Senado, then head southwest, roughly on the well-signposted Historic Centre

Above from far left: Macau is gambling central; European-style architecture.

Gambling on Macau

Macau has long been the only place in China where casinos are legal, much to the delight of Hong Kong residents. In 2002 local tycoon Stanley Ho's four-decade monopoly of the gaming industry ended, and Las Vegas and foreign casino operators entered the market. Reclamation around the Macau peninsula, and most dramatically between the islands of Taipa and Coloane, provided land for the tiny enclave to expand, and the one billion people across the border with a passion for gambling, increasing incomes and a new freedom to travel guaranteed big winnings.

In 2006 Macau earned more from gambling than Las Vegas; today there are over 30 casinos. Wynn Macau, Sands Macau and MGM Macau have joined Ho's former flagship Casino Lisboa and his new 40-storey Grand Lisboa on the Macau peninsula. Taipa's casinos include the amusing Greek Mythology Casino, but the most astonishing expansion is on the Cotai Strip (see p.87). In 2007 the largest building in Asia, The Venetian Macao Resort Hotel, opened with 3,000 guest rooms, 850 gaming tables, 4,100 slot machines, over 350 stores in a 'baroque mall' and Zaia, a permanent Cirque du Soleil show.

The global financial crisis slowed development, but Macau is still going strong. In 2009 the glitzy City of Dreams opened with vast luxury hotels and fanastic theatre shows.

Above from left: Macau-Taipa Bridge; fish drying in the sun.

Below: the magnificent preserved façade of São Paulo (St Paul's; *see pp.88–9*).

of Macau Trail; at the peninsula's tip is **Barra** ❻, a fort that was the site of the first Portuguese settlement on Macau. It's an easy walk, along sleepy streets that suggest the Mediterranean far more than Nevada. There are a dozen or so churches, buildings and squares from the 17th, 18th and 19th centuries along the way.

Located just past the end of the Calcada da Barra is the **A-Ma Temple** ❼ (daily 7am–6pm), above the **Porto Interior** (Inner Harbour), which predates the Portuguese arrival. Nearby, the **Maritime Museum** ❽ (Wed–

Mon 10am–5.30pm; charge) traces the history of seafaring on the South China Sea. Some of Macau's best restaurants, especially for traditional Macanese cuisine, face the water along **Rua Almirante Sérgio**, such as **A Lorcha** and **O Porto Interior**, see ⑪④ and ⑪⑤.

NAPE

A hub of hectic socialising on the Macau peninsula is **Nape** ❾, a rectangular grid of streets on reclaimed land on the east of town near the ferry terminal. As well as a proliferation of casinos it contains a number of bars and the **Centro Cultural de Macau** ❿, which also has a stylish bar and restaurant. Nape is also home to the copper-toned **Wynn Macau**, the glistening **MGM Grand** and the giant luxury-brand mall and residential development **One Central**. Get a taste of Vegas in Asia by visiting one or more of them, or alternatively just catch a taxi back to the ferry pier.

Food and Drink

④ A LORCHA
289 Rua Almirante Sérgio, Macau; tel: 2831 3193; $$
One of Macau's best for Portuguese-Macanese cuisine: try pork with clams or *feijoada* (pork-and-bean stew). Very popular, so book ahead.

⑤ O PORTO INTERIOR
259 Rua Almirante Sérgio, Macau; tel: 2896 7770; $$
Delicious Macanese classics in an attractive, cosy restaurant.

MACAU: TAIPA AND COLOANE

Take time to explore the contrasts of old and new Macau in the islands of Taipa and Coloane with their placid old villages, linked by southern China's new Las Vegas in the Cotai Strip.

For most of their history the two islands south of Macau city that make up the rest of the territory, **Taipa** and **Coloane**, were sleepy colonial backwaters. Since the 1970s, though, bridges have bound them to Macau and the Chinese mainland, while the channel between them has been filled by a land reclamation scheme, **Cotai**, that now hosts the biggest bangs in Macau's gambling boom.

> **DISTANCE** Varies – see map
> **TIME** A full day
> **START** Museum of Taipa and Coloane History, Taipa
> **END** Coloane
> **POINTS TO NOTE**
> Minibuses 21A, 25 and 26A run between Macau, Taipa and Coloane. Taipa and Coloane can be explored on foot, but you'll need to take a taxi or bus to get between them via Cotai.

OLD TAIPA

Minibuses from Macau stop in the middle of Taipa Village. Begin a tour at the **Museum of Taipa and Coloane History** ❶ (Tue–Sun 10am–6pm; charge), near the bus stop on Rua Correia da Silva, in a 1920s mansion once used by the islands' council. The Portuguese only gained control over Taipa and Coloane in the mid-19th century, and even in the early 1900s rugged Coloane was known as a pirates' lair. Exhibits illustrate Taipa's old trades of boat-building, fishing and firework-making, and the islands' mix of Western and Chinese religions and architecture.

When you're ready to see more, step out into old Taipa. Across the road at the junction of Correia da Silva and Rua Governador Tamagnini Barbosa is a small **Tin Hau Temple**, built in 1785. From here head east along Rua Correia da Silva and turn left to reach **Largo dos Bombeiros** ❷, Taipa's cobbled village square, with its 1920s **market** building. The narrow streets around the square are lined with quaint old Chinese shops, Portuguese-style painted houses and Buddhist shrines and temples. **Rua da Cunha** is packed with restaurants and Chinese food shops: for enjoyable Portuguese snacks, try **O Santos**, *see p.93*, ⑪①.

Carmel and Taipa's Old Mansions
On a small hill east of the square is **Our Lady of Carmel** ❸, a primrose-

Taipa Flea Market
If you are in Taipa on a Sunday, visit the bustling weekly flea market (11am–8pm), which is held on Largo dos Bombeiros. Stalls sell items including traditional handicrafts, toys, clothing and shoes, factory over-runs and souvenirs.

Above from left:
Macau fishing boats;
Portuguese-style
egg-custard tarts.

Venice in China
From the Taipa
Houses Museum it's
only a ten-minute
walk to the
gargantuan Venetian
Macao, opened in
mid-2007. Combining
a hotel, casino,
shopping mall, sports
venue and conference
centre, all on a vast
scale, it's a major
attraction all by itself.
There are lots of
refreshment options
too. From Chinese-
Portuguese Macau
you are suddenly in
a candy-coloured
version of Italy,
walking around
St Mark's Square or
visiting the 350 shops
along the Grand
Canal, under a 24-
hour blue sky. Hitch a
ride on a gondola with
singing gondolier for
MOP$120, or head
to the vast expanses
of the casino floor.
Other options include
watching the Cirque
du Soleil's *Zaia*
show, which plays
here permanently.

and-white church from 1885. Walk past the market building, and turn right up the banyan tree-lined steps to get there. From the top of the steps you will have your first clear view of **Cotai**, the reclaimed land that now joins Taipa to Coloane, and the sea of cranes and scaffolding of casinos and hotels under construction. Over to your left is **Macau International Airport**; behind that is **Taipa Temporary Ferry Terminal**.

From Our Lady of Carmel walk down the hill to **Avenida da Praia**. Before reclamation ships used to moor along the waterfront here, lined by the pretty homes of prosperous Macanese merchants. Five of these jade-green and white mansions, built in the 1920s, have been restored as **Taipa Houses Museum ❹** (Casa-Museu da Taipa; Tue–Sun 10am–6pm; free). Two are used for temporary exhibitions, and three house permanent displays on Macau history and traditions, which charmingly re-create life in Portuguese and Chinese homes in the colony before its boom. The Avenida is now a peaceful, tree-lined promenade, and the old harbour is a closed-in, lotus-covered pond, across which you can't miss the vast constructions of Cotai.

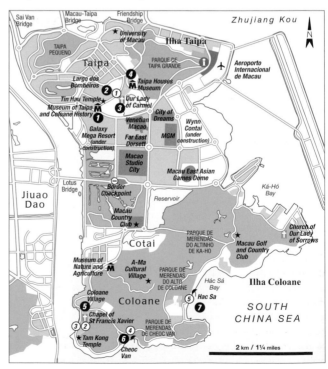

COLOANE

Head back to Largo dos Bombeiros to get a taxi or bus on to **Coloane**. What was once the last hiding place for South China Sea pirates is now a green retreat from the SAR's bustle, casinos and construction, with hills, beaches and Macau's only country park. Its resident population still live in small villages around the former island's shores, and mostly in **Coloane Village ⑤** itself, on the western side.

Around the Village

Get off the bus at the roundabout of Largo Presidente Antonio Ramalho. Walk down **Rua Dos Negociantes** to the tiny **Chapel of St Francis Xavier**, built in 1928 to commemorate the recapture by the Portuguese of some children snatched by pirates in 1910 and held for ransom on Coloane. It looks onto a tiny village square, which comes alive with restaurant tables on weekends and holidays. The **Nga Tim** is also open all week, see ⑪②.

From the square you can explore the maze of Coloane's lanes, where you will find a few small shops selling antique and reproduction furniture. For a light snack, look out for **Lord Stow's Bakery**, see ⑪③. A short walk from the south end of the square is the **Kun Iam Temple**, built in 1677 and dedicated to the gods and goddesses of heaven, war, wealth, medicine and carpenters. Then walk south along the restored waterfront, facing China, to the **Tam Kong Temple** (1862), which has a dragon boat carved from a whale bone by the local fishermen as a gift for Tam Kong.

Coloane's Beaches

To see more of Coloane, head back to Largo Ramalho and catch a bus to **Cheoc Van ⑥**, where there's an open-air pool next to a white sandy beach. Get off when you see the sign for the **Pousada de Coloane**, and kick back with a long cold drink at **La Gondola** by the pool, see ⑪④. Alternatively, go on to **Hac Sa ⑦** (Black Sands), which despite its colour is Coloane's most popular beach, and has its best-known restaurant, **Fernando's**, see ⑪⑤. When you're ready, the restaurant staff will be able to call you a taxi to go back to Macau.

Coloane's Peak

If the weather is not too hot, tackle the half-hour hike uphill through pine woods, from Cheoc Van beach to the A-Ma Cultural Village, near Coloane's highest point. Though most of this complex has been built recently, in style it follows those of shrines from the Qing dynasty: dominated by a 20m (65ft) A-Ma (Tin Hau goddess), which can be seen from the sea. Free shuttle buses run from the peak to the main road into Coloane.

Food and Drink 🍴

① O SANTOS
20 Rua da Cunha, Taipa; tel: 2882 5594; $–$$
Football memorabilia on the walls confirms you've found the right place. Stuffed pork loin and curried crab are house specialities.

② NGA TIM CAFÉ
8 Rua Caetano, Coloane Village; tel: 2888 2086; $
Eat alfresco on Coloane's beautiful village square. Delicious Portuguese and Macanese dishes, including grilled chorizo, garlic prawns and African chicken.

③ LORD STOW'S BAKERY
1 Rua da Tassara, Coloane Village; tel: 2888 2534; $
Well known for its excellent *pasteis da nata* (Portuguese egg tarts) and also good for fresh bread, snacks and coffee.

④ LA GONDOLA
Praia Cheoc Van, Coloane; tel: 2888 0156; $$
Spend an afternoon by the beach, then move to La Gondola's terrace for pizzas, seafood or salads with Portuguese wines.

⑤ FERNANDO'S
Hac Sa Beach, Coloane; tel: 2888 2531; $$–$$$
Mainly Portuguese menu, with lots of seafood: excellent prawns in clam sauce. No reservations; fans wait in the bar in the garden.

DIRECTORY

A user friendly alphabetical listing of practical information,
plus hand-picked hotels and restaurants, clearly organised
by area, to suit all budgets and tastes. Select nightlife listings
are also included here.

A

ADDRESSES

Hong Kong is a multistorey city. The ground floor is G/F, the one above 1/F (first floor), and so on. However, the address may also be written '205' (for second floor, apartment 5). Many buildings are referred to by their name as well as the street address, as in *1/F Sanlitun Causeway Centre, 28 Harbour Road*.

Many taxi drivers speak English, but ask your hotel to write addresses for you in Chinese, just in case they don't.

B

BUSINESS CARDS

In business affairs in Hong Kong, you will be expected to present a business card. Present them to a Chinese person with both hands, and accept them the same way.

C

CHILDREN

Most five-star hotels offer a babysitting service. **Rent-a-Mum** (www.rent-a-mum.com) is a well-established agency that can arrange short-term help with babies and children.

CLIMATE

Hong Kong is just south of the Tropic of Cancer, and has a subtropical climate divided into four seasons:

• **Winter**: Between late December and February, the weather generally varies from mild to cool, with some fog and rain. Temperatures average between 13°C (55°F) and 20°C (68°F). However, they can occasionally dip down to below 10°C (50°F).

• **Spring**: The period from March to mid-May sees a mix of damp, overcast weather and pleasant sunny days. Temperatures range from a daytime average of 20°C (68°F) in March to 28°C (82°F) in May. Humidity is usually high.

• **Summer**: Temperatures and humidity rise from late May to mid-September, as the southwest monsoon blows in from equatorial Asia. The weather is marked by hazy, humid heat, punctuated by dramatic rainstorms and the odd clearer day. Temperatures usually rise above 30°C (86°F), and 80–90 percent humidity is not uncommon; the mercury scarcely drops at night. August and September are peak typhoon months.

• **Autumn**: One of the most pleasant times to visit Hong Kong. The northeast monsoon usually takes over by October, bringing cooler, drier air from the mainland. From late September, temperatures drop from 29°C (84°F) to around 20°C (68°F) in December. Humidity is generally quite low.

CLOTHING

During the hottest months you will want to wear the lightest clothes possible. Shorts, T-shirts and comfortable shoes or sandals are essential, especially if you aim to spend a lot of time out-

doors. Bring a light sweater or jacket for over-air-conditioned buildings. If you envisage attending local social occasions, or want to sample Hong Kong's more glittering nightlife, bring something cool but elegant too, not just a T-shirt and jeans *(see margin right)*.

Temperatures can vary sharply from one day to the next from November to April, so pack for warm and cool days, and dress in layers to peel off or put back on. Few buildings have heating, so it can seem colder inside than out.

CRIME AND SAFETY

One of the joys of Hong Kong is the low level of crime. In the main shopping and entertainment areas men and women can walk alone pretty safely at any hour of the day, and most of the night. Tourists may be more obvious targets for pickpockets in busy areas, but normal basic precautions usually suffice.

Macau is also a safe destination, but more caution is advisable in Shenzhen, where muggings and a few other incidents have been reported. Dress down to visit Shenzhen, and leave your jewellery behind. Stick to busy areas, and when shopping, do not let the lure of a bargain make you forget common sense.

CONSULATES AND VISA OFFICES

Australia: Consulate-General, 23–24/F Harbour Centre, 25 Harbour Road, Wan Chai; tel: 2827 8881; www.australia.org.hk.

Canada: 11/F Tower 1, Exchange Square, 8 Connaught Place, Central; tel: 2810 4321; www.hongkong.gc.ca.
Ireland: Honorary Consul, Heidrick & Struggles, 54/F Bank of China Tower, 1 Garden Road, Central; tel: 2527 4897; www.consulateofireland.hk.
New Zealand: 6501 Central Plaza, 18 Harbour Road, Wan Chai; tel: 2525 5044; www.nzembassy.com/hongkong.
UK: Consulate-General, 1 Supreme Court Road, Central; tel: 2901 3000; www.britishconsulate.org.hk.
USA: Consulate-General, 26 Garden Road, Central; tel: 2523 9011; http://hongkong.usconsulate.gov.

Mainland China

Office of the Commissioner of the Ministry of Foreign Affairs, 5/F Lower Block, China Resources Building, 26 Harbour Road, Wan Chai; tel: 3413 2300. Visa applications to visit the mainland are made at the **Visa Office** (Seventh Floor). Two photos are required. Single-entry visas cost from HK$250 to HK$400 (depending on your nationality) and are processed in one to three days. China visas can also be obtained through all the Hong Kong Offices of the **China Travel Service** (CTS), 78 Connaught Road, Central; tel: 2853 3888, www.ctshk.com, and from many Hong Kong travel agents.

CUSTOMS

Visitors aged 18 and above can import almost anything for their personal use (including an unlimited amount of cash), but 60 cigarettes (or 15 cigars/

75g of tobacco) and one litre of spirits. For further details, see www.customs.gov.hk.

Hong Kong has stringent restrictions on the import and export of ivory and other items from endangered species protected by the CITES convention. There are also strict controls on meat, firearms and weapons (which must be declared on arrival and handed in for safe-keeping), narcotics and fireworks.

D

DISABLED TRAVELLERS

With the exception of the airport, big hotels and some newer large buildings, Hong Kong is not easy for travellers with disabilities to navigate. A useful guide to public buildings and attractions, *The Hong Kong Access Guide for Disabled Visitors*, is available at www.hkcss.org.hk/rh/accessguide or from HKTB (Tourist Board) Information Centres, and a full guide to transport facilities is on the Transport Department website, www.td.gov.hk. Taxis are often the easiest way to get around, but **Easy Access Travel** has a fleet of adapted buses, which can be chartered (www.easyaccesstravelhk.com).

E

ELECTRICITY

The Hong Kong electrical system runs at 200/220 volts and 50 cycles AC. Most plug sockets take British-style three-pin plugs. When purchasing electronics of any kind, always check that the system and power requirements are compatible with your systems at home.

EMERGENCY NUMBERS

General emergencies: 999 (for police, fire service or ambulance)
Police Enquiries: 2527 7177
Hospital Authority: 2300 6555

F

FURTHER READING

Non-Fiction

Booth, Martin. *Gweilo: Memories of a Hong Kong Childhood*. An affectionate memoir of growing up in the 1950s.
Endacott, G.B. *A History of Hong Kong*. Long considered the 'Bible' of Hong Kong history, an exhaustive study of the former British colony.
Patten, Christopher. *East and West*. An insider's account of the handover of Hong Kong to China in 2007 by the last British Governor.
Porter, Jonathan. *Macau: The Imaginary City*. Readable study of Macau's history and its commercial and cultural relationship with China.
Tsang, Steve. *A Modern History of Hong Kong, 1841–1997*. Full account of Hong Kong history and the emergence of a Hong Kong identity.

Fiction

Clavell, James. *Taipan*. The rise of a British merchant clan in 19th-century

Hong Kong. The sequel *Noble House* takes the story into the 20th century.
Gardam, Jane. *Old Filth*. A former Hong Kong judge looks back on his rootless colonial life.
Han Suyin. *A Many Splendoured Thing*. Set in Hong Kong, the story of the author's love affair with a western correspondent during the Korean War.
Le Carré, John. *The Honourable Schoolboy*. The shady world of Le Carré's Cold War reaches Hong Kong.
Mason, Richard. *The World of Suzie Wong*. The book that made Wan Chai and its bar girls famous, as an English artist falls in love with a local girl. A convincing picture of 1950s Hong Kong.
Mo, Timothy. *An Insular Possession*. Set during the Opium War, the backdrop to Britain's seizure of Hong Kong.
Xi Xi. *Marvels of a Floating City* and *A Girl Like Me and Other Stories*. Stories from a leading Hong Kong writer.

H

HEALTH

No vaccinations are required to enter Hong Kong, but doctors often recommend immunisations against hepatitis A and B, flu, polio and tetanus. Tap water exceeds WHO standards, but bottled water may be more palatable and is widely available. For current information on influenza and other health concerns, see www.who.int/csr/en.

Medical Services

All visitors are strongly advised to take out adequate travel health insurance before arriving, to cover emergencies and all other possible medical expenses. Hong Kong does not have a free national health care system, and visitors are required to pay at least HK$570 if they use the Accident & Emergency services at public hospitals. Listed below are some hospitals with 24-hour A&E services. For more information on all medical services, call the Hospital Authority helpline, tel: 2300 6555, or visit www.ha.org.hk.

Hospitals

Caritas Medical Centre: 111 Wing Hong Street, Sham Sui Po, Kowloon; tel: 3408 7911.
Prince of Wales Hospital: 30–32 Ngan Shing Street, Sha Tin, New Territories; tel: 2632 2211.
Queen Elizabeth Hospital: 30 Gascoigne Road, Kowloon; tel: 2958 8888.
Queen Mary Hospital: 102 Pok Fu Lam Road, near Aberdeen, Hong Kong Island; tel: 2855 3838.

Pharmacies

Conventional pharmacies (identified by a red cross) are abundant, as are traditional Chinese herbalists. Pharmacies will only accept prescriptions issued by a doctor in Hong Kong.

HOLIDAYS

Hong Kong's public holidays are a happy mixture of traditional Chinese, Christian and political feast days. Banks, offices, post offices and some shops will all be closed on the following days:

Above from far left: temple offerings; lions guarding a Hong Kong art gallery.

Taking the Air
Air pollution is a constant concern, and Hong Kongers often blame this on the boom in Guangdong. However, Hong Kong produces plenty of pollutants by itself, and owns many of the factories over the border. A joint plan between Hong Kong and Guangdong province is intended to cut emissions, but so far results have been limited. Asthma sufferers are often affected by pollution in urban Hong Kong, but in most of the New Territories and islands the air is noticeably fresher. A daily air pollution index and a wide range of other environmental information can be found on the website of the Hong Kong government: www.gov.hk.

Extending Holidays
If a festival falls on a Sunday, or two festivals coincide, the day preceding or following the festival is usually also designated as a general holiday.

1 January: New Year's Day
Late January/February: Chinese (Lunar) New Year, a three-day holiday
March/April: Good Friday and Easter Monday
March/April: Ching Ming Festival
April/May: Buddha's Birthday
1 May: Labour Day
June: Tuen Ng (Dragon Boat) Festival
1 July: Hong Kong Special Administrative Region Establishment Day
September: the day following the Mid-Autumn Festival
1 October: China National Day
October: Chung Yeung Festival
25 December: Christmas Day. The 26th, or the first weekday after Christmas Day, is also a holiday.

HOURS

Offices generally open Monday to Friday 9am–5.30pm or 6pm, but some government offices open from 8.30am–4.30pm. Many business offices also work a half day (9am–1pm) on Saturdays. Banks are open Monday to Friday 9am–4.30pm, Saturday 9am–12.30pm.

Mall shopping tends to go on between 10am and 9pm, but the major shopping districts of Causeway Bay and Tsim Sha Tsui stay open later, till 10 or 11pm. Smaller local shops, especially for food, open earlier, at 8–9am, and each market is different: some open mainly in the morning, while others, such as Yau Ma Tei's famous Temple Street night market, don't get going until well after lunch.

Most shops open every day of the year, except during Chinese New Year.

Reading the Street
All street signs are in English and Chinese, and Hong Kong street maps usually have both an English and a Chinese-language section in the back, to make it easier to find where you're going. Sometimes the English name of a street or district is simply a transliteration of the Chinese name, but in many other cases the Chinese name is totally different and may have no visible relation to the English one.

ID

Hong Kong residents are required to carry an identity card. Visitors are advised to carry with them a similar form of photo identification, such as your passport or a photocopy of it.

INTERNET

All hotels provide internet access though most charge for in-room service. Free wireless broadband access (WiFi) is becoming more widespread all the time in hotels, and the government is building a free city-wide GovWiFi network. You can also access the web for free at PCs in many coffee shops.

L

LANGUAGE

Hong Kong's official languages are Chinese and English. Street names, public transport and utilities signage and government publications are bilingual, as are most notices and menus. Most major institutions have bi- or even trilingual voicemail systems.

The predominant language of street-level Hong Kong is Cantonese (Guangdonghua), a regional Chinese dialect also spoken in Guangzhou and the surrounding Guangdong province. Many organisations post announcements and information in Cantonese, English and Mandarin (Putonghua), China's 'national' language. English is still the

language of international business, and most people who come into contact with visitors speak at least a smidgen.

M

MAPS

HKTB Information Centres *(see p.103)* carry an extensive range of maps and give them to visitors on arrival. The General Post Office, 2 Connaught Road, has a good choice of maps and guides in its ground-floor gift shop.

MEDIA

Newspapers and Magazines

The South China Morning Post is the dominant English-language newspaper. The tabloid-style *Standard* is free and focuses on local business. Hotel bookshops, newspaper vendors at the Central Ferry Piers, Star Ferry TST and branches of Bookazine and Dymocks bookshops all usually have a good selection of international newspapers and magazines.

Television

Hong Kong has four terrestrial TV stations, ATV World and TVB Pearl in English and ATV Home and TVB Jade in Cantonese. Most programmes on the English-language stations are US shows or movies; not much is produced locally in English except for news. Most hotels offer a mix of cable and satellite channels including CNN, BBC World, Discovery, ESPN, National Geographic, TNT and HBO.

Radio

Hong Kong's main radio station RTHK relays 24-hour news from the BBC World Service on its RTHK6 channel (675 kHz AM), and there's also news in English on local station Metro Plus (1044 kHz AM).

For classical music, tune to RTHK4 (97.6–98.9 mHz FM); pop and easy listening are on RTHK3 (567 and 1584 kHz AM/97.9 and 106.8 mHz FM) and 104 FM Select (104 mHz FM). For round-the-clock contemporary music try HMV AM (864 kHz AM).

MONEY

The currency unit is the Hong Kong Dollar, which is pegged to the US dollar at around US$1 = HK$7.80. In spring 2010 HK dollar exchange rates were HK$11.70 to £1 sterling or HK$10.40 to €1.

Bank notes are issued by HSBC, Standard Chartered Bank and the Bank of China in the following denominations: HK$1,000, HK$500, HK$100, HK$50, HK$20 and the plasticised HK$10. Coins include HK$10, HK$5, HK$2, HK$1, 50 cents, 20 cents and 10 cents.

Hong Kong dollars are interchangeable with the Macau currency, the Patacca (MOP). In Shenzhen, Lo Wu stores will accept Hong Kong dollars and convert to Renminbi (RMP) on the spot, but taxis and other retailers want to be paid in RMP, so it may be worth changing your money before crossing the border In spring 2010, HK$1 = RMB 0.88.

Tipping

Most restaurants and hotels add a 10 percent service charge to bills automatically. It's also common practice to round up restaurant bills to the nearest HK$10, and larger gratuities are expected when no service charge has been added. Taxi fares, too, are often rounded up to the nearest dollar or two as a sufficient tip. Restroom attendants and doormen can be tipped in loose change, and HK$10–20 is enough for bellboys and room service in most hotels.

Traveller's Cheques

Banks, hotels and money changers accept traveller's cheques. Banks generally offer the best rates to change them (also foreign currency), although most charge commission.

Credit Cards and ATMs

Visa, MasterCard, American Express and other major cards are accepted at most hotels, restaurants and shops. However, check the cash price in shops; it may be lower than for card purchases. In most street markets, only cash is accepted. When using cards, check that the total is filled in correctly, and keep the customer's copy.

Cash Machines (ATMs) are plentiful. Visa and MasterCard holders can get HK dollars from Hang Seng Bank and HSBC cash machines; American Express cardholders can access Jetco ATMs.

P

POST

The Hong Kong mail is fast and efficient. Stamps are normally bought at post offices, most of which open Mon–Fri 9am–5pm, and Sat mornings. Airmail stamps are also available at 7-11 and Circle-K convenience stores.

The best places for sending packages and registered mail are the General Post Office (2 Connaught Place, Central; Mon–Sat 8am–6pm) and the large Kowloon post office (10 Middle Road, Tsim Sha Tsui; Sun 8am–2pm). For more information, tel: 2921 2222, or visit www.hongkongpost.com.

T

TELEPHONES

Public telephone kiosks, although not as common as they once were, can still be found all around Hong Kong – the easiest places to find them are MTR stations, 7–11 stores and hotel and bank lobbies. The standard charge for using a pay phone is HK$1 per five minutes for local calls. However, Hong Kong landline local calls are free, so you can usually use a phone in a shop or restaurant for no charge. (Note, though, that many hotels charge for local calls from your hotel room.)

You can make international calls direct from pay phones with a credit card or stored-value phone card (available at HKTB Information Centres, 7–11s and some bookshops). To make a call outside Hong Kong, dial the international access code, 001, followed by the country code and number. Within Hong Kong, there are no area codes and all numbers have eight digits, except for toll-free numbers, which begin with 800, and some public information numbers, which begin with 18 or 10.

Mobile (Cell) Phones

Hong Kongers love their cell phones. Most providers' phone systems (GSM 900, PCS 1800, CDMA, WCDMA) operate in Hong Kong. To avoid roaming charges, it's a good idea to get a prepaid SIM card with a Hong Kong number and fixed number of minutes. Many phone providers and convenience stores sell SIM cards.

文武廟
Man Mo Temple

孫中山紀念館
Dr Sun Yat-sen Museum

Telephone Codes

Hong Kong from abroad **852**

Macau **853**

Mainland China **86**

Shenzhen **86 755**

Useful Phone Numbers

Hong Kong Directory Enquiries: **1081**

International Directory Enquiries: **10013**

International Operator/Collect calls: **10010**

Hong Kong International Airport Information, in English (24 hours): **2181 0000**

Weather Information: **187 8200**

TIME

Hong Kong is eight hours ahead of GMT and 13 hours ahead of US Eastern Time. Unlike in Europe and the US, there is no daylight saving time, so from April to October the difference is reduced to seven hours ahead of London and 12 ahead of New York.

TOURIST INFORMATION

The Hong Kong Tourist Board (HKTB) has booths at the airport, at ferry piers and at land crossings just after you clear customs. They offer free HKTB information packs, which contain a map, a current-events magazine, brochures and details of tourist-board-organised day and half-day tours. They also run an excellent multilingual visitor hotline, tel: 2508 1234 (daily 8am–6pm), and have a great website: www.discoverhongkong.com.

Other useful websites include:

- **Hong Kong SAR Leisure and Culture Department**: www.lcsd.gov.hk.
- **Macau Tourist Office**: www.macautourism.gov.mo.

HKTB Information Centres

Hong Kong International Airport: Transfer Area E2 and Buffer Halls A and B, Arrivals Level, Terminal 1; daily 7am–11pm.

Hong Kong Island: Causeway Bay MTR station (exit F); daily 8am–8pm.

Kowloon: Star Ferry Concourse, Tsim Sha Tsui; daily 8am–8pm.

TRANSPORT

The high-rise jungles of Hong Kong may look daunting, but this is an easy city to get around, thanks to a highly efficient, easy-to-use public transport system. To make the most of it (and save money), use an Octopus travel card or a Transport Pass *(see pp.104–5)* rather than single tickets. Children aged under 11 travel half-fare on most transport, and under-3s travel free.

Arriving by Air

Hong Kong International Airport (HKIA) is at Chek Lap Kok, on the north shore of Lantau Island about 34km (21 miles) from Central, which, as its name suggests, is the urban heart of Hong Kong Island. Immigration queues are dealt with swiftly, and suitcases are often circling the carousel by the time you reach the baggage hall.

Airport Information: tel: 2181 0000; www.hongkongairport.com.

Checking in on the Airport Express
Travellers leaving Hong Kong can check in their luggage at the airline counters at the Airport Express stations at Hong Kong Central and Kowloon up to a full day before their flight time (depending on which airline you are flying with).

Tours

The HKTB offers a varied mix of tours, bookable from its Information Centres (see p.103). Other attractive options include: New World First Bus's day's unlimited hop-on hop-off rides (HK$50 per day) on its two open-top Rickshaw Bus routes on Hong Kong Island (www. nwstbus.com,hk). HeliExpress (tel: 2108 9898; www. helihongkong.com) offer day and night sightseeing tours by helicopter. Hong Kong Dolphinwatch (tel: 2984 1414; www.hkdolphin watch.com) runs regular half-day trips to see the Pearl River's endangered dolphins off Lantau. Saffron Cruises (tel: 2857 1311; www. saffron-cruises.com) has Chinese junks and other boats for hire. Watertours of HK (tel: 2926 3868; www.watertours. com.hk) offer a choice of nine harbour cruises in delightfully gaudy boats, in the morning, afternoon or by night.

Transport To and From the Airport

All transport to the city leaves from the Ground Transportation Centre, well signposted from the Arrivals Hall. The Airport Express rail line, part of the MTR system (see opposite), is the quickest and most convenient, but not the cheapest, way into town. All trains now run to and from the AsiaWorld-Expo exhibition site beside the airport as well as from the Transportation Centre, and reach Central station in just 23 minutes, with stops at Tsing Yi and Kowloon.

Trains run in both directions daily 5.50am–1.15am, every 12 minutes. Tickets to Central cost HK$100 single, HK$180 return, to Kowloon HK$90 single, HK$160 return, but note that you can already use an Octopus card (see below) to save money from the airport.

Airport Express connects with the MTR at Tsing Yi and Central. Free shuttle buses also run between Central and Kowloon Airport Express stations and many hotels, Hung Hom KCR train station and the China Ferry Terminal. Passengers can check in bags at Airport Express stations up to two hours before departure.

There are also airport buses, which run to every part of Hong Kong and the New Territories. Airbus services, prefixed A, run to various destinations, and there are also slower, still cheaper 'commuter' buses (prefixed E). A11 and A12 run through the busiest parts of Hong Kong Island, A21 through Kowloon. Airbus fares to the city range between HK$33–45, while E-route fares are HK$14–24. Route details are posted at the Transportation Centre.

There are also shuttle buses to Tung Chung station on the main MTR, which is cheaper than Airport Express. Night buses from the airport (prefixed N) mostly run 0.20–5am.

Taxis are easy to find, at the rank outside the Ground Transportation Centre. Urban taxis are red; New Territories taxis are green; local Lantau taxis are blue. A taxi to Central on Hong Kong Island will cost around HK$340, to Kowloon slightly less; all fares from the airport include HK$30 toll for the Lantau island road bridge.

Arriving by Sea

Macau and a handful of cities in Guangdong, China are connected to Hong Kong by ferry. Hong Kong is also a starting-off or end point to a large number of cruise itineraries. For now, cruise ships dock at the **Ocean Terminal** in Tsim Sha Tsui, right next to the Harbour City mall. A new cruise terminal is due to open in 2013 at the site of the former airport at Kai Tak.

Getting Around: Travel Passes

The **Octopus card** is a smart card, valid on all kinds of transport except taxis and some minibuses and ferries. It can be bought at MTR stations, the airport and tourist information centres. You pay a deposit of HK$50 for the card, then charge it up (minimum HK$150). You swipe the card on special machines each time you board a train, bus, tram, etc, and the fare is deducted; once your initial amount runs out, you can recharge the card at machines at MTR stations, 7–11 and Circle-K convenience stores,

Above from far left: on the bus; Hong Kong International Airport.

as well as supermarkets, which also accept payment by Octopus. For details, see www.octopuscards.com.

Tourist Passes are a more limited option than the Octopus. The **MTR 1-day Tourist Pass** gives you a day's unlimited travel on the MTR for HK$50; the 3-day **Transport Pass** gives you three days' travel on the MTR and some bus routes, including one (HK$220) or two (HK$300) Airport Express trips. Both types of pass are available from Airport Express and MTR stations and tourist information centres.

Getting Around: The MTR

The Mass Transit Railway (MTR) is a fast, efficient, clean, air-conditioned rail network that runs daily from around 6am to 12.30/1am. As well as the Airport Express, it has ten lines *(see inside back cover for map)*. Adult single fares range from about HK$4 to HK$26. All stations have automatic machines where you can buy tickets or recharge your Octopus card *(see left)*. There are no toilets at stations or on trains, and smoking, eating and drinking are forbidden throughout the MTR.

MTR stations are well signposted in English and Chinese; on the train, each stop is announced in Cantonese, Mandarin and English. Most stations have several exits, identified by letters and numbers, so it's useful to have an idea of which you want; however, there are good local area maps at all stations, and lists of major nearby buildings and roads by all station exits. For more information, tel: 2881 8888 or visit www. mtr.com.hk.

Getting Around: Buses

Bus routes, run by several companies, cover every part of the SAR, but are most handy for areas not on MTR or rail lines, such as the south side of Hong Kong Island and much of the New Territories. Most run 6am–midnight, but some operate all night, and night buses run on several other routes.

Most city buses are British-style double-deckers. Drivers rarely speak much English, but each stop has route maps and timetables in English and Chinese. Non-Octopus fares range from HK$1.20 to HK$45. Note that drivers do not carry change, so if you don't have an Octopus card or a Transport Pass *(see left)*, you must have the exact change.

Many routes begin from or run via one of four large termini: at the Central Ferry Piers, beneath Exchange Square and by Admiralty MTR on Hong Kong Island, and the Star Ferry Concourse in Tsim Sha Tsui.

Bus Information

You can pick up free **maps** of main bus routes at HKTB Information Centres. **Citybus**: tel: 2873 0818: www.citybus. com.hk. **Discovery Bay Transportation Services**: tel: 2987 0208; www.hkri.com. **Kowloon Motor Bus (KMB)**: tel: 2745 4466; www.kmb.com.hk. **Long Win Bus Company**: tel: 2261 2791; www.kmb.com.hk. **New Lantao Bus Company**: tel: 2984 9848. Serves all of Lantau. **New World First Bus**: tel: 2136 8888; www.nwfb.com.hk. City routes, and many to the New Territories.

Taxi Tips

Many taxi drivers speak some English, but some exchanges can be challenging. Ask someone at your hotel desk to write your destinations down in Chinese; also, all cabs are equipped with radio phones, and somebody at the control centre should be able to translate. Drivers will also sometimes refuse a fare if the journey will take them out of their way as they are about to finish work; rather than try to argue, it is usually better just to find another taxi.

Getting Around: Minibuses

Sixteen-seater minibuses are another option: 'red' minibuses (they are actually cream-coloured, but with a red stripe) run on fixed routes in the city, and 'green' minibuses (cream with a green stripe) run to many small destinations, especially in the New Territories.

Destinations are usually written in English at the front of the van; minibuses stop anywhere, so call out clearly when you want the driver to stop (try *lee do* in Cantonese). Fares vary from HK$1.50 to HK$20. On red minibuses, you pay as you get out, and drivers do not usually have much change, though on some routes you can use Octopus cards. Exact change or an Octopus card are needed for green minibuses.

Getting Around: Trams

Trams have rattled all the way along the north side of Hong Kong Island since 1904, and the double-decker carriages are a great-value means of seeing the city. Stops are frequent, and you can hop on and off as you please.

The flat fare is HK$2 (HK$1, under-12s and over 65s); exact change is required, or use the Octopus card or a Transport Pass *(see pp.104–5)*. Trams run daily 6am–1am. You get on at the back and get off at the front, paying as you get off. Avoid lunchtimes and rush hours, and head up to the front of the top deck.

The **Peak Tram** is actually a funicular railway, up to the Peak Tower *(see p.54)*. **Hong Kong Tramways**: tel: 2548 7102; www.hktramways.com. **Peak Tram**: tel: 2522 0922; www.the peak.com.hk.

Getting Around: Star Ferries

These green and white, open-sided little ferries run back and forth between the Central Ferry Piers (Piers 7 and 8) and Wan Chai on Hong Kong Island and Tsim Sha Tsui and Hung Hom in Kowloon. They run daily 6.30am–11.30pm, every 6–12 minutes, and the trip takes about eight minutes. Octopus cards are valid. At HK$2.20 (upper deck) and HK$1.70 (lower deck), Central to Tsim Sha Tsui is one of the cheapest scenic ferry rides in the world. **Star Ferry Information**: tel: 2367 7065; www.starferry.com.hk.

Getting Around: Taxis

Taxis are abundant and easy to hail on the street, outside rush hours. Taxis come in three colours: red on Hong Kong Island and Kowloon, green in the New Territories and blue on Lantau.

Hong Kong taxis are cheap: minimum fare for red cabs is HK$18, with extra charges for luggage placed in the car boot, booked cabs, and tunnel and bridge tolls. All fares are metered, and receipts given. By law passengers must wear seat belts, and drivers will remind you if you don't buckle up straight away. To call for a cab, tel: 2571 2929.

Ferries to the Outlying Islands

Ferries to Lamma, Lantau and Cheung Chau leave from Piers 3, 4, 5 and 6 of the Central Ferry Piers, near the Star Ferry Piers in Central on Hong Kong Island. Two types operate on most routes: standard ferries and slightly more expensive fast ferries.

Standard ferries are slower but have outdoor decks with great views.

New World First Ferry has the most routes. Fares vary greatly (and may be slightly more at weekends and holidays) but start from HK$11. Octopus cards can be used on most ferries; otherwise, take the correct money, as change booths are only open at peak times. If visiting Lamma, be aware that there are two routes: one to Yung Shue Wan, the other to Sok Kwu Wan.

Outlying Islands Ferry Information
Discovery Bay Transportation Services: tel: 2987 0208; www.hkri.com. Ferries to the south side of Lantau.
Hong Kong Kowloon Ferry: tel: 2815 6063; www.hkkf.com.hk. To Lamma.
New World First Ferry: tel: 2131 8181; www.nwff.com.hk. Runs to most of the islands.

*Ferries to Macau
and Mainland China*
Turbojet (tel: 2859 3333; www.turbo jet.com.hk) runs ferries 24 hours a day, 365 days of the year to Macau from the Shun Tak Centre's Macau Ferry Terminal, west of the Central Ferry Piers, and China Ferry Terminal in Tsim Sha Tsui, Kowloon. *See p.87.* Cotai Jet ferries (www.cotaijet.com. mo) run from the same locations in Hong Kong to the ferry terminal on Taipa. Turbojet also runs direct ferries to Macau from Hong Kong Airport, and less-frequent ferries from China Ferry Terminal to ports in Mainland China, and from the Airport to Shenzhen.

*Trains to the New Territories
and Mainland China*
The MTR network *(see p.105)* includes four lines serving the New Territories. Trains are fast and frequent: every 3–10 minutes, 5.30am to 12.30–1am daily, and the full trip on East Rail takes 42 minutes, on West Rail 30 minutes. Fares cost HK$4.50– $36.50, and you can use Octopus cards. Many stations are hubs for local bus routes. MTR Information: tel: 2881 8888; www.mtr.com.hk

There are trains roughly once an hour daily, 7.30am–7.15pm, from Hung Hom station in Kowloon to Guangzhou via Shenzhen. There are also long-distance trains to Beijing or Shanghai every two days. If direct tickets to Guangzhou are sold out, take the East Rail line to the border at Lo Wu. The Shenzhen station is a few minutes' walk across the border.

V

VISAS

Most visitors only need a valid passport to enter Hong Kong. The length of tourist visit normally allowed varies by nationality: British citizens with full UK passports are given six months; nationals of other EU countries, Australia, Canada, New Zealand, the US and some other countries get three months. If in doubt, see the Hong Kong Immigration website, www.immd.gov.hk.

When you arrive, your passport must be valid for at least a month beyond your planned date of departure.

Hong Kong has some of the world's best hotels, with suitably high prices to match levels of luxury and standards of service that are consistently rated at the top of the world league. Leading hotel groups including Peninsula, Mandarin Oriental, Shangri-La and Langham all have their roots in Hong Kong, and international chains such as Hyatt and InterContinental all have flagship properties here in the SAR.

Hong Kong's spectacular big hotels are city landmarks, used by locals as much as by visitors – for dining, meeting and socialising. There is no official star-rating system for hotels in Hong Kong, but, while scarcity of land means that bedrooms are often somewhat on the small side, the quality of the restaurants, spas and other extra services, ambience and general opulence of the city's top-line hotels is difficult to beat.

Hong Kong also now has a few smaller-scale boutique hotels – with similar prices to the hotel giants – and luxury serviced apartments are another option. However, even if you are not travelling on a hefty expense account, there is still a good choice of mid-range hotels around the city.

> Price bands based on standard rates for a double room per night, without breakfast.
>
> $$$$ over HK$2,500
> $$$ HK$1,400–HK$2,500
> $$ HK$750–HK$1,400
> $ under HK$750

Hong Kong Island

Bishop Lei International House

4 Robinson Road, Mid-Levels; tel: 2868 0828; www.bishopleihtl. com.hk; $$

An excellent-value option – owned by the Catholic Diocese of Hong Kong – located 15 minutes' walk from the nightlife hub of Lan Kwai Fong, and with SoHo on its doorstep via the Mid-Levels Escalator. There's nothing remarkable about the decor, but it offers many of the facilities of an upper-range hotel – including a gym, pool, free in-room broadband, 24-hour room service and babysitter and concierge services – at exceptionally reasonable prices. Some suites even have impressive harbour views.

The Emperor (Happy Valley) Hotel

1a Wang Tak Street, Happy Valley; tel: 2893 3693; www.emperorhotel. com.hk; $$

Tucked away near Happy Valley racecourse, but still only five minutes' walk from Causeway Bay, this relatively small (for Hong Kong) 150-room hotel is nowhere near the height of Hong Kong chic – rooms are old-fashioned plush – but very comfortable, and extremely good value. There's a courtesy shuttle bus to the main business districts.

The Excelsior

281 Gloucester Road, Causeway Bay; tel: 2894 8888; www.excelsior hongkong.com; $$$

Around 200 of the Excelsior's 884 rooms have partial or full harbour views across to Kowloon, and overlooking the colourful Causeway Bay typhoon shelter. Part of the Mandarin Oriental Group, this is a huge but friendly upper-mid-range hotel with efficient service and a pleasant environment, close to Causeway Bay's shopping district and the MTR.

The Fleming

41 Fleming Road, Wan Chai; tel: 3607 2288; www.thefleming. com.hk; $$–$$S

When location is everything this 66-room boutique hotel in the middle of the Wan Chai commercial and nightlife district does the trick. The stylish rooms are compact yet cosy and packed with gadgets. Thoughtful touches include a female-only floor and free access to California Fitness next door.

Grand Hyatt Hong Kong

1 Harbour Road, Wan Chai; tel: 2588 1234; www.hongkong. grand.hyatt.com; $$$$

The glitziest hotel in Hong Kong welcomes you with gold and marble at every turn, creating luxury on a palatial level. A top location overlooking the harbour and alongside the Hong Kong Convention and Exhibition Centre gives fabulous views from most of its 549 elegant rooms. The hotel's many other features include the superior Tiffin Lounge and Champagne bar – one of HK's most chic rendezvous – and the fabulous Plateau Spa, with every kind of beauty and fitness treatment on offer, as well as an outdoor pool.

The Harbourview

4 Harbour Road, Wan Chai; tel: 2802 0111; www.theharbourview. com.hk; $$$

Affiliated to the YMCA, this smart mid-range hotel – one of Hong Kong's surprising bargains – targets business and leisure travellers, with well-equipped, comfortable rooms and an ultra-convenient Wan Chai location very near the Hong Kong Arts Centre. It's worth paying the extra HK$100 for a room with a view of the harbour, but book early, as it's very popular.

Hotel Jen

508 Queen's Road West, Sheung Wan, Western District; tel: 2974 1234; www.hoteljen.com; $$

A comfortable, excellent-value mid-range hotel in the oldest district on Hong Kong Island. Great views from the rooftop pool and swish Sky Lounge on the 28th floor. It's 10 minutes' drive from Central, but a courtesy shuttle bus is provided to the MTR and Airport Express stations.

Hotel LKF

33 Wyndham Street, Lan Kwai Fong; tel: 3518 9333; www. hotel-lkf.com.hk; $$$–$$$$

One of the city's hippest addresses, on Wyndham Street, right in the middle of Lan Kwai Fong. The sleek, minimalist rooms have espresso machines and DVD players, and guests can avail themselves of a whole range of services.

Above from far left: business silhouette *(left)* and hotel chic *(right)* at the excellently priced Harbour View.

Taxes and Charges
A 10 percent service charge is added on to nearly all hotel bills in Hong Kong. It is not usually included, though, in the published list prices, so take this into account when budgeting.

Dining facilities include the original FINDS Scandinavian-based restaurant, and a very sexy 29th-floor cocktail bar and supper lounge, AZURE. Great hotel, although note that the streets outside can be noisy into the small hours.

Island Shangri-La Hong Kong

Pacific Place, Supreme Court Road, Central; tel: 2877 3838; www. shangri-la.com; $$$$

A soaring 17-storey atrium is only one of many spectacular features of the Shangri-La group's flagship, 565-room property. Rooms are more than usually spacious, with large bathrooms, a big range of electronic gadgets (including broadband and DVDs) and stunning panoramic views views of the harbour or the Peak. The restaurants are highly regarded by local gourmets, whether the refined Cantonese cuisine of the Summer Palace or the modern fusion-fare of the elegantly romantic Petrus. Free broadband access.

Jia

1–5 Irving Street, Causeway Bay; tel: 3196 9000; www.jiahongkong.com; $$$–$$$$

The stylish, urbane Jia was Hong Kong's first boutique hotel, with lots of the hall-marks of designer Philippe Starck. The 54 studio-rooms are compact, but stunning to look at – and the electronics and other services are really state of the art. Complimentary breakfast, afternoon cakes, cocktail-hour wines, gym access and excellent service also make the Jia surprisingly good value.

Jockey Club Mount Davis Youth Hostel

Mount Davis Path, Victoria Road, Western District; tel: 2788 1638; www.yha.org.hk; $

Spartan accommodation but superb views are offered at this famous hostel, with its mountain-top location at the westernmost end of Hong Kong Island, above Kennedy Town and Pok Fu Lam. It's ever-popular with back-packers and hard to beat for value, but you will be required to join in chores. A 30-minute shuttle bus takes you to Shun Tak Centre and Macau Ferry Terminal, from where you are just five minutes from Central.

JW Marriott Hong Kong

Pacific Place II, 88 Queensway, Central; tel: 2810 8366; www. jwmarriotthk.com; $$$$

A smart, quality hotel with six restaurant choices including the fun Fish Bar, next to the Marriott's great city pool with its dramatic views of Hong Kong's skyscrapers. All of the 602 well-sized rooms have some view of the harbour, and there's direct access to Pacific Place mall and Admiralty MTR.

Lan Kwai Fong Hotel

3 Kau U Fong, Sheung Wan; tel: 2311 6280; www.lankwaifong hotel.com.hk; $$$

A relatively low-key, boutique-style hotel, with a great location – actually west of the real Lan Kwai Fong district, but not far from Hollywood Road, Man Mo temple and SoHo. There's in-house dining and internet access, and five

In Season

Hong Kong's high seasons are in October–November and March–April, when business people from around the world flock to trade shows and exhibitions, but the months between these times, including Christmas and Chinese New Year, can also be very busy. At other times, it's easier to find a big choice of rooms available, and you're more likely to be offered discounted prices.

suites have balconies (almost unheard of in Hong Kong) with spectacular views across Central to the harbour. Very good value among Hong Kong's high prices.

Mandarin Oriental Hong Kong

5 Connaught Road, Central; tel: 2522 0111; www.mandarin oriental.com; $$$$

A Hong Kong institution, where the local movers and shakers meet and celebrities stay, lured by impeccable service, superb facilities and some of the finest hotel dining in an already well-served town. The Mandarin reopened at the end of 2006 after a major refit, with larger rooms than before and state-of the art gadgets; it still retains, though, its traditional charm. The Mandarin Oriental's famed restaurants and bars include the Conran-revamped Mandarin Grill and the legendary Captain's Bar and Chinnery bar.

Novotel Century Hong Kong

238 Jaffe Road, Wan Chai; tel: 2598 8888; www.novotel.com; $$

Extremely convenient branch of the Novotel chain in the heart of Wan Chai, within easy reach of the MTR, the arts venues around the Convention Centre and Wan Chai nightlife. The hotel's ample facilities include a health club and an outdoor pool.

Park Lane

310 Gloucester Road, Causeway Bay; tel: 2293 8888; www.parklane.com.hk; $$$

Understated and relaxing 802-room hotel, where the bustle of Causeway Bay's shopping zones is balanced out by the green expanse of Victoria Park and the quieter streets towards the Peak. The best rooms have fine harbour views.

The Wharney Hotel

57–73 Lockhart Road, Wan Chai; tel: 2861 1000; www.gdhhotels.com; $$

A medium-sized, recently built hotel in the middle of the Wan Chai commercial and nightlife district, with extensive facilities that include an outdoor pool. One oddity is that, although it's part of a hotel group based in mainland China, it has a Scottish theme bar, the 'Canny Man', promising a choice of over 100 whiskies.

Kowloon

Anne Black YWCA

5 Man Fuk Road, Ho Man Tin; tel: 2713 9211; www.ywca.org.hk; $$

The YWCA offers clean, simple and spacious rooms at bargain rates in a fairly quiet part of Kowloon, still only a short walk from the Ladies' Market, Jade Market and Mong Kok KCR and MTR stations. Rooms are available to both women and men, but there is a women-only floor.

Price bands based on standard rates for a double room per night, without breakfast.

$$$$	over HK$2,500
$$$	HK$1,400–HK$2,500
$$	HK$750–HK$1,400
$	under HK$750

Above from far left: checking in at the Park Lane; executive room at the Island Shangri-La.

Most of Hong
Kong's upscale
hotels now offer
broadband connec-
tions in every room,
usually for an extra
charge, as wel as
free WiFi in public
areas. Many mod-
est hotels in Hong
Kong, Macau and
China simply offer
free WiFi. It's worth
checking when
booking, as new
internet connec-
tions may not be
mentioned in a
hotel's published
advertising.

BP International House

8 Austin Road, Tsim Sha Tsui; tel:
2376 1111; www.bpih.com.hk; $$$
Owned by the Scouts, this hotel enjoys
a marvellous location, in the heart of
Tsim Sha Tsui near Kowloon Park.
Standard bedrooms are plain but
comfortable, although the BP's spe-
ciality is its big choice of room types,
from dormitory-style bunk rooms to
corporate suites.

Chungking House

4–5/F, Block A, Chungking
Mansions, 40 Nathan Road,
Tsim Sha Tsui; tel: 2366 5362;
www.chungkinghouse.com; $
Chungking Mansions is a labyrinth of
a building that's home to around 4,000
people, many in 'guesthouses' that have
long been a first port of call for budget
travellers. Some find the place exciting,
others are overwhelmed. Chungking
House is far and away the best of its
guesthouses, the only one to win the
HKTB's seal of approval. Rooms are
plain, small but clean, all have bath-
rooms, and they're still ultra-cheap.
They're on the fourth and fifth floors,
so there's no need to use the scary lifts.

Eaton Hotel Hong Kong

380 Nathan Road, Yau Ma Tei;
tel: 2782 1818; www.eaton-hotel.
com; $$
Extremely pleasant hotel with facilities
and service above the norm for this price
range – including WiFi and a rooftop
swimming pool. The emphasis is on
contemporary styling and good value,
and prices are very competitive. Well
located for Temple Street night market,
shops, cinemas and Jordan MTR.

InterContinental Hong Kong

18 Salisbury Road, Tsim Sha Tsui;
tel: 2721 1211; www.hongkong-ic.
international.com; $$$$
One of Hong Kong's most glamorous
hotels, with perhaps the best harbour
views in town from its grandstand posi-
tion on the Tsim Sha Tsui waterfront,
minutes from the Star Ferry. The Inter-
Continental exudes luxury, and its
Lobby Bar and rooftop infinity spa
pools are not to be missed. Its superb
collection of restaurants is for some the
city's finest, with a Nobu outlet, Spoon
by French superchef Alain Ducasse
and the ever-popular Steakhouse.

Kowloon Hotel

19–21 Nathan Road, Tsim Sha Tsui;
tel: 2929 2888; www.harbour-plaza.
com; $$$
An elegant modern business hotel that
soars up behind The Peninsula in the
heart of Tsim Sha Tsui's commercial and
entertainment district. There's no pool
or health club – hence the lower-than-
usual prices – but guests can use the
sister property Harbour Plaza Metrop-
olis or pay HK$120 to use the upmarket
YMCA in the next block. Watch out for
its competitive promotional offers.

Kowloon Shangri-La Hotel

64 Mody Road, Tsim Sha Tsui East;
tel: 2721 2111; www.shangri-la.com;
$$$$
Grand and quietly confident, the
Kowloon Shangri-La offers a full range

of facilities including a large indoor pool and highly rated restaurants. It's on the east side of Tsim Sha Tsui, but convenient for transport links to the New Territories and the mainland. Free broadband access.

Langham Hotel

8 Peking Road, Tsim Sha Tsui; tel: 2375 1133; www.langham hotels.com; $$$$

Classic styling, sumptuous decor and a choice of seven high-standard restaurants – Cantonese, contemporary Asian-fusion, American and more – are the trademarks of this opulent hotel, a snug, restrained haven which is equidistant from the MTR, the Star Ferry and the China Ferry Terminal.

Langham Place Hotel

555 Shanghai Street, Mong Kok; tel: 3552 3388; www.hongkong. langhamplacehotels.com; $$$$

The Langham Place is part of a multi-purpose office and leisure complex that rises like a shiny new incisor from a once run down patch of Mong Kok. It prides itself on its use of technology, and the hi-tech rooms have gadgets such as guest phones that can be taken anywhere in the hotel, WiFi, huge plasma screens and DVDs, as well as floor-to-ceiling windows over a fascinatingly vibrant district of Hong Kong. The softer side of the hotel is seen in its displays of contemporary art, a heated rooftop pool and the fabulous Chinese-themed Chuan spa.

Marco Polo Hong Kong Hotel

Harbour City, 3 Canton Road, Tsim Sha Tsui; tel: 2113 0088; www.marcopolohotels.com; $$$$

A deluxe hotel with unrivalled advantages for devoted shoppers, as it's actually part of the giant Harbour City shopping and leisure complex by Tsim Sha Tsui's Ocean Terminal. The ample facilities include an outdoor pool and three fine restaurants. Also hosts a massively popular Oktoberfest on the TST waterfront each year.

Metropark Hotel Mongkok

22 Lai Chi Kok Road, Mong Kok; tel: 2397 9622; www.metropark hotels. com/mongkok; $$

Formerly known as the Concourse, this big hotel offers no special features but good-value comfort, and is popular with Asian business travellers and groups. It's in the heart of Mong Kok near Prince Edward MTR, and close to Fa Yuen Street's factory outlets.

The Mira

118 Nathan Road, Tsim Sha Tsui; tel: 2368 1111; www.themirahotel. com; $$$

After a US$65-million makeover in 2009, the colourful, youthful and very stylish Mira is one of the many reasons Tsim Sha Tsui's glitz factor is on the rise. Facilities include the acclaimed restaurants Whisk (European) and Cuisine Cuisine (Cantonese), as well as an indoor infinity pool and spacious soothing spa in the basement.

Above from far left: InterContinental Hong Kong; Langham Hotel.

Web Browsing
Several locally based websites offer very good package deals on hotels in Hong Kong, Macau and the Mainland, often together with flights and other services. Websites worth checking include www.asiatravel.com, www.asiahotels. com, www.wotif. com and www. ctrip.com.

Hong Kong may be best known for giant, glittering luxury hotels, but another feature of the city is the intriguing number of mid-range hotels and hostels that are owned by churches and other charitable institutions, such as the Bishop Lei International House, owned by the Catholic Church, and the various YMCAS or YWCAS, such as the Salisbury, the Anne Black or, a star in the field, the Harbour View. These places frequently offer comforts and extras – even pools and WiFi – that wouldn't be out of place in an upper-mid-range hotel. Hence, they rank among Hong Kong's top bargains.

Nathan Hotel

378 Nathan Road, Yau Ma Tei; tel: 2388 5141; www.nathanhotel. com; $$–$$$

This quiet, pleasant mid-range hotel is located close to the Temple Street Night Market and Jordan MTR, and has 180 spacious and well-decorated no-frills rooms that have recently been renovated. The Penthouse restaurant serves Cantonese and Western food, and there's also a Starbucks coffee shop on site.

The Peninsula

Salisbury Road, Tsim Sha Tsui; tel: 2920 2888; http://hongkong. peninsula.com; $$$$

Hong Kong's most historic, most prestigious hotel has been a byword for impeccable service and colonial-style grandeur since it opened in 1928, and Noël Coward was only one of the globetrotting celebs who stayed here in its first golden era. Today, one only has to step into the magnificent lobby, where the celebrated afternoon tea is served, to imbibe the ambience of yesteryear. However, the Peninsula also has its feet firmly in the present: it was extensively refurbished in the 1990s, with a new 30-storey tower, and rooms are the pinnacle of luxury, matching the hotel's helipad and fleet of Rollers – with legendary views from the famous corner-suite baths. In-house restaurants include Gaddi's, for many Hong Kong's best French restaurant, and the Philippe Starck-designed Felix top-floor bar, with its men's loo with a view.

Salisbury YMCA

41 Salisbury Road, Tsim Sha Tsui; tel: 2268 7000; www.ymcahk.org.hk; $$

Book well ahead to be sure of a room at this superior YMCA. Rooms, which are divided between singles, family rooms and dormitories, are plain but comfortable and well equipped, and many of them enjoy panoramic views of the harbour and Hong Kong Island's nightly 'Symphony of Lights'. Amenities include a large indoor pool and impressive sports facilities. As conveniently located as 'The Pen' (see left), but at a fraction of the cost.

Sheraton Hong Kong Hotel and Towers

20 Nathan Road, Tsim Sha Tsui; tel: 2369 1111; www.sheraton.com/ hongkong; $$$$

Lively luxury hotel with an ample range of facilities including an outdoor pool with superb views of Hong Kong Island, a Fitness First-managed gym and 'Harbour View' rooms where you can enjoy fabulous views while lying back in your bath. Restaurants and bars include a Casa del Habano cigar bar and the top-floor Sky Lounge.

Shenzhen

Mission Hills Resort

Guanlan County; tel: (86 755) 2802 0888; www.missionhillsgroup.com; $$$$

A very opulent resort that's part of the world's largest golf complex, which has 12 designer courses, pools and any amount of other sporting facilities.

Shangri-La Hotel Shenzhen

East Side, Railway Station, Jianshe Lu; tel: (86 755) 8233 0888; www.shangri-la.com/shenzhen; $$$$

One of few real landmarks in Shenzhen, the Shangri-La has long held the crown of 'best hotel in town'. The location is ultra-convenient, the food is consistently excellent, the gardens offer a pleasant escape and the 360° bar has great views. Free broadband.

Macau

Altira Macau

Avenida de Kwong Tung, Taipa, Macau; tel: (853) 2886 8888; www.crown-macau.com; $$$$

Exquisite bedrooms by award-winning designer Peter Remédios with great views of Macau, and a fabulous infinity pool in an enormous spa: the Altira is a class apart from the more hectic Macau casino hotels, and located slightly away from the main clusters. Restaurants offer contemporary French, Japanese and Chinese cuisine.

Mandarin Oriental Macau

Avenida da Amizade; tel: (853) 2856 7888; www.mandarinoriental.com/macau; $$$–$$$$

The brand-new Mandarin Oriental Macau opened in 2010 as part of the huge luxury shopping, residential and commercial complex, One Central. The 213-room property has all the usual Mandarin Oriental comforts, technology and superb service. No casino on site, but MGM Macau, Wynn Macau and the Grand Lisboa are all within walking distance.

Pousada de Coloane

Praia de Cheoc Van, Coloane; tel: (853) 2832 8144; www.hotelpcoloane.com.mo; $$

Quiet, family-run hotel by the beach. Decor is rustic Portuguese, with blue-and-white wall tiles and terracotta tiles on the floor. A lovely place to relax, eat home-style Portuguese food and enjoy the views of Cheoc Van beach.

Pousada de Sao Tiago

Avenida da Republica; tel: (853) 2837 8111; www.saotiago.com.mo; $$$$

A great change from Macau's Las Vegas-style projects, this romantic luxury hotel occupies a 17th-century fort, fittingly decorated with dark woods and marble. The garden pool and terrace are lovely, and historic Macau is just outside.

Westin Resort Macau

Estrada de Hac Sa, Coloane; tel: (853) 871 111; www.westin-macau.com; $$$$

The Westin Resort Macau is definitely the hotel for golfers, with a lift up to the first tee on the hotel's roof. It's handy too for the beach and Fernando's restaurant. A luxurious escape from the downtown crowds.

Price bands based on standard rates for a double room per night, without breakfast.

$$$$	over HK$2,500
$$$	HK$1,400–HK$2,500
$$	HK$750–HK$1,400
$	under HK$750

Staying in Macau and the Mainland

Prices in Macau are generally less than those for a hotel of the same standard in Hong Kong; in Shenzhen and elsewhere on the Mainland prices are lower still. Good deals on Macau hotels are often available online and from Hong Kong travel agents. If you can, avoid trying to stay in Macau on a weekend – above all Saturday night – when huge numbers of Hong Kongers nip across for a night's gambling. On any other night of the week rooms in Macau are both cheaper and easier to find.

RESTAURANTS

Food is an integral part of the Hong Kong experience. *Yum cha* – eating *dim sum* and drinking tea – is a must, as is dining alfresco on one of the outlying islands. *Cha chen tengs* (casual cafés/diners) and *dai pai dongs* (outdoor street-side restaurants) such as those around Temple Street are also unique to the SAR. Dining in shopping malls is also very typical of Hong Kong life; most malls have a mix of both medium- and lower-priced restaurants and food courts, where you order from any of over a dozen outlets, and then eat at a communal table. Some of the best deals to be had at top restaurants are their set menus, especially at lunchtime. The dining areas listed below are packed with places offering great 'lunch sets', which allow you to indulge for a lot less than the à la carte price.

Central and the Peak
Cuisine Cuisine
3101–07, Level 3, IFC Mall, Finance Street; tel: 2393 3933; www.cuisine cuisine.hk; Mon–Fri noon–2.30pm, 6–10.30pm, Sat–Sun 11am–3pm, 6–10.30pm; MTR: Central; $$$
Set in a huge, high-ceilinged, highly designed space with indoor and out-

door dining and magnificent views, this Michelin-starred restaurant showcases contemporary Cantonese cuisine with refined modern touches. A second restaurant has opened in The Mira Hotel, Nathan Road *(see p.113)*.

FINDS
2/F Lan Kwai Fong Tower, 33 Wyndham Street; tel: 2522 9318; www.finds.com.hk; Mon–Fri noon–midnight, Sat 7pm–3am, Sun 10.30am–5.30pm; MTR: Central; $$$
An acronym of Finland, Iceland, Norway, Denmark and Sweden, FINDS has a menu that offers a mix of specialities from the Nordic region. It is also a very cool place to dine, with a fabulous wooden deck for pre-dinner cocktails and a great location at the top of vibrant Lan Kwai Fong. Service is attentive, and the quality high.

Good Luck Thai Food
G/F 13 Wing Wah Lane; tel: 2877 2971; Mon–Sat 11am–2am; MTR: Central, then Mid-Levels Escalator; $–$$
Cheap, cheerful dining at plastic tables in a pungent but authentic Hong Kong alleyway just off the bar and nightlife hub of Lan Kwai Fong. Come here to feast tom yam soup, phad thai and other Thai favourites.

Habibi
1/F, Grand Progress Building, 15 and 16 Lan Kwai Fong; tel: 2544 6198; www.habibi.com.hk; Mon–Sat 11.30am–11.30pm; MTR: Central; $$–$$$

Price guide for an average three-course meal for one with a glass of wine:

$$$$	over HK$500
$$$	HK$300–HK$500
$$	HK$150–HK$300
$	below HK$150

Habibi is like a Cairo-esque bazaar from the 1930s, with high ceilings, dazzling mirrors, hubble-bubble pipes and even belly dancers. Serving authentic, delicious Egyptian food, it does a great-value two-course set lunch. Specialities include Egyptian mixed grill and cold meze, all prepared by an Egyptian chef (and all halal). Similar dishes are available deli-style, and cheaper, at the Habibi Café at 112–114 Wellington Street. Both highly recommended.

Jashan

1/F Amber Lodge, 23 Hollywood Road; tel: 3105 5300, www.jashan.com.hk; Mon–Sat noon–3pm, 6–11pm; MTR: Central, then Mid-Levels Escalator; $–$$

Richly decorated, Jashan offers an extensive menu of Indian cuisine, with dishes from north and south. A speciality is the exceptional-value lunch buffet. Fine dining in the evening.

Kiku Japanese Restaurant

Basement, Gloucester Tower, The Landmark, Des Voeux Road East; tel: 2521 3344; daily 11.30am–3pm, 6–10.30pm; MTR: Central; $$$

A traditional, pine-panelled restaurant serving teppanyaki and sushi delicacies, kaiseki, or sukiyaki or shabu-shabu set meals. The à la carte menu features Kyoto-style cuisine; great grilled cod and eel.

Life Organic Health Café

10 Shelley Street; tel: 2810 9777; www.lifecate.com.hk; Mon–Fri 8am–midnight (meals served noon–10.30pm), Sat–Sun 10am–midnight (meals served 10am–10.30pm); MTR: Central, then Mid-Levels Escalator; $$

A popular vegetarian café and restaurant, where health-conscious locals munch on freshly baked flapjacks and alfalfa, in between sips of freshly squeezed passion fruit and carrot juice.

Above from far left: stylish bar; cakes; healthy wrap; fresh oysters.

Left: Indian dish at Jashan.

Luk Yu Tea House

24–6 Stanley Street; tel: 2523 1970; daily 7am–10pm; MTR: Central; $–$$

This popular, famous tea house opened in the early 1930s. With its carved wood panelling and doors, ceiling fans, spittoons, marble tabletops, couples booths and stained-glass windows it is fabulously atmospheric. A great place to try the full range of Chinese teas. Also famed for its excellent dim sum (served until 5.30pm). Ask for the English menu.

Mandarin Grill

Mandarin Oriental Hotel, 5 Connaught Road, Central; tel: 2825 4004; www.mandarinoriental.com; MTR: Central; $$$$

One of Hong Kong's best-loved grills, the Mandarin has benefited from a Terence Conran makeover. Although the menu is pricey, the Grill is sublime and worth every penny. You may never taste steak this good (fish, pasta and sushi also on the menu) or be treated to such finely tuned service. Book well in advance.

Ning Po Residents Association

4/F Yip Fung Building, 10 D'Aguilar Street, Lan Kwai Fong; tel: 2523 0648; daily noon–2.45pm, 6–10.45pm; MTR: Central; $$

Hidden away inside a commercial building, this dazzlingly lit, clattering, local-style restaurant offers a vast range of dishes from Shanghai and Ningpo in northeast China.

Qing

3 Mee Lun Street; tel: 2815 6739; Mon–Sat 11.30am–11.30pm; MTR: Central, then Mid-Levels Escalator; $$

Contemporary Vietnamese tapas, in the NoHo (North of Hollywood Road) area. Qing has a comfortable bar and an outdoor terrace, and good set lunch menus for about HK$80.

Va Bene

17–22 Lan Kwai Fong; tel: 2845 5577; www.vabeneristorante.com; Mon–Thur noon–2.30pm, 6.30–11.30pm, Fri noon–2.30pm, 6.30pm–midnight, Sat 6.30pm–midnight, Sun 6.30–11pm; MTR: Central; $$$$

Located in the heart of bustling Lan Kwai Fong, the sleek, fashionable Va Bene is one of the city's most enduringly popular dining spots. It offers trattoria-style cuisine from northern Italy, in pleasant surroundings.

Wan Chai and Causeway Bay

IR 1968 Indonesian Restaurant

28 Leighton Road, Causeway Bay; tel: 2577 9981; daily 11.30am–11.30pm; MTR: Causeway Bay; $$

The original restaurant opened here back in 1968, hence the name. It has

Price guide for an average three-course meal for one with a glass of wine:

$$$$	over HK$500
$$$	HK$300–HK$500
$$	HK$150–HK$300
$	below HK$150

since had a major face-lift and is now a funky joint decorated in deep reds and browns. The food is tasty too, with Indonesian favourites from *nasi goring* and *gado* to delicious beef and cuttlefish curries.

The Pawn

2/F and 3/F 62 Johnston Road, Wan Chai; tel: 2866 3444; www.thepawn.com.hk; Living Room Mon–Sat 11am–2am, Sun 11am–midnight; Dining Room noon–3pm, 6pm–midnight; MTR: Wan Chai, $–$$$

Four traditional shop houses were saved from the wrecker's ball and converted into this beautiful venue with original features from local pawn shops. Food in the second-floor Dining Room is modern British. Those in the know, though, order bar snacks such as a ploughman's lunch and park themselves in huge wicker chairs on the balcony of the first-floor Living Room and watch the Wan Chai world go by.

Red Pepper

G/F 7 Lan Fong Road, Causeway Bay; tel: 2577 3811; 11.30am–3pm; 5.30pm–midnight; MTR: Causeway Bay; $$–$$$

This long-established Sichuan restaurant serves up authentic fiery dishes in icy air conditioning. For the cautious, the menu has helpful chilli symbols to indicate how hot the dishes are. For fans of spicy food, Red Pepper's sizzling prawns are a must. No faux retro here: the decor is much as it was in the 1970s.

La Cuisine de Mekong

2/F, 15 Knutsford Terrace, Tsim Sha Tsui; tel: 2316 2288; www.mhihk.com; daily 6pm–3am; MTR: Tsim Sha Tsui; $$

This restaurant does spicy sauces, soups, grilled-meat salads, stir-fries and exotic desserts that represent the cuisines of the Mekong region: southwest China, Burma, Laos, Cambodia, Thailand and Vietnam. The decor reflects French colonial times, and there is an outdoor 'garden' surrounded by tropical palms.

Fat Angelo's

Shop B, Basement, The Pinnacle, 8 Minden Avenue, Tsim Sha Tsui; tel: 2730 4788; www.fatangelos.com; daily noon–midnight; MTR: Tsim Sha Tsui; $$

A friendly, uncomplicated, American Italian-style restaurant dishing up huge portions of pasta that can feed up to eight people. Children get an activity menu, but later on it can also be a romantic setting, with its checked tablecloths and wine served in tumblers. There are five more branches around Hong Kong and the New Territories.

Gaylord

1/F Ashley Centre, 23–5 Ashley Road, Tsim Sha Tsui; tel: 2376 1001; www.chiram.com.hk; daily noon–2.30pm, 6.30–11pm; MTR: Tsim Sha Tsui; $$$

This Kowloon institution has been around since 1972 and serves North

Above from far left: ready for business at Life *(see p.117)*; tantalising menu; dim sum; thousand-year-old eggs.

and South Indian cuisine, with plenty of seafood and vegetarian dishes. The decor is rather on the bland side, but live music is a nightly feature and the lunch and dinner buffet menus offer good value for money.

Her Thai

Shop 1, Promenade Level Tower 1, China Hong Kong City, 33 Canton Road, Tsim Sha Tsui; tel: 2735 8898; daily noon–11pm; MTR: Tsim Sha Tsui; $$

Offering reasonably priced, enjoyable Thai food, this modest restaurant also has fabulous views of the harbour, taking in the Central skyline. The interior, with its gentle lighting and red hanging lanterns, is one of Hong Kong's most romantic settings.

Jimmy's Kitchen

1/F Kowloon Centre, 29 Ashley Road, Tsim Sha Tsui; tel: 2376 0327; www.jimmys.com; daily 11.30am–3pm, 6–11.30pm; MTR: Tsim Sha Tsui; $$

Wood-panelled Jimmy's is one of Hong Kong's oldest restaurants, which has been in business since the 1930s; it now has a street-level restaurant. It specialises in British and European food but also does curries and a variety of other Asian dishes. There is also a branch in the South China Building, 1–3 Wyndham Street in Central, tel: 2526 5293.

The New Sangeet

Shop Nos UG06–08, Toyo Mall, Intercontinental Plaza, 94 Granville Road, TST East; tel: 2367 5619;

daily noon–3pm, 6–11pm; MTR: Tsim Sha Tsui; $$$

'Sangeet' means music in Hindi, and that is exactly what you will find each evening after 8pm, when a Bhangra band plays Indian classics (Indian classics also grace the menu). The decor is modern, however, with moody blues and purples, couches bedecked with cushions, and a certain Bollywood glamour pervading the restaurant.

Nha Trang

Shop OT G51, Ground Floor, Ocean Terminal, Harbour City, Tsim Sha Tsui; tel: 2199 7779; www.nhatrang.com.hk; daily noon–11pm; MTR: Tsim Sha Tsui; $

Low prices and dishes bursting with flavour from spices and herbs make this an enjoyable, refreshingly reasonably priced place to feast on Vietnamese cuisine. Recommended dishes include the addictive *pho* noodle soup, fresh rice paper rolls with grilled prawns, crispy skinned suckling pig, and minced pork on lemon grass sticks. Service is patchy, but that doesn't seem to deter the punters. Other branches in Central and Wan Chai are equally good, but this one has the harbour view.

Price guide for an average three-course meal for one with a glass of wine:	
$$$$	over HK$500
$$$	HK$300–HK500
$$	HK$150–HK300
$	below HK$150

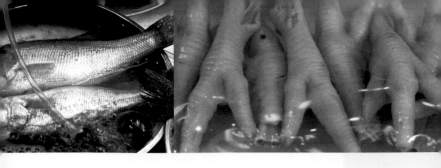

Nobu

Intercontinental Hong Kong,
18 Salisbury Road, Tsim Sha Tsui;
tel: 2313 2323; www.hongkong-ic.
intercontinental.com; daily noon–
2.30pm, 6–11pm; MTR: Tsim Sha
Tsui; $$$$

Huge views of the harbour and city skyline are on a par with the bluefin at the famed sushi-meister's first Asian venture outside Japan. The waiting list is long, but if you fail to bag a table try the small sushi bar with its nine non-bookable stools, or retreat with sake Martinis to the lounge bar, which shares the same vistas.

Ruth's Chris Steakhouse

Empire Centre, 68 Mody Road,
Tsim Sha Tsui East; tel: 2366
6000; www. ruthschris.com;
daily noon–3pm, 6.30–11pm;
MTR: Tsim Sha Tsui; bus: Salisbury
Road; $$$$

If you are a carnivore craving a juicy steak, this American chain, serving cuts of fillet, strip, rib-eye, porterhouse and T-bone, should hit the spot. Other mains include tuna, chicken, lamb chops and lobster, and salads and sandwiches are also available. Another branch is in the Lippo Centre, 89 Queensway, Central, tel: 2522 9090.

Sorabol Korean Restaurant

4/F Miramar Shopping Centre,
1 Kimberley Road; Tsim Sha Tsui;
tel: 2375-2882; MTR: Tsim Sha Tsui;
$$

One of Hong Kong's best Korean restaurants, serving authentic dishes that draw in the local Korean community. Barbecue at your table or order à la carte. If there's a queue – and there often is – make a booking, then head to Knutsford Terrace for a drink while you wait.

Spice Market

3/F Marco Polo Prince Hotel,
Harbour City, 23 Canton Road,
Tsim Sha Tsui; tel: 2113 6046;
www. marcopolohotels.com;
daily 6am– 10.30pm; MTR: Tsim Sha
Tsui; $$$

Do not be put off by the hotel location: this is a pleasant, relaxed restaurant presenting a wide variety of Asian foods, including Japanese, Chinese, Thai and Indian specialities, hotpots, satays and more. Buffets are the order of the day, so this is a great option if you are not sure what you feel like, want to pick and mix or if you have fussy children in tow. It is also accessible from the Gateway mall.

Spring Deer

42 Mody Road, Tsim Sha Tsui East;
tel: 2366 4012; daily noon–3pm,
6–11pm; MTR: Tsim Sha Tsui; bus:
Salisbury Road; $$

There is nothing fancy about Spring Deer, but this Beijing-style restaurant is a local institution for Peking duck, lamb and other northern specialities, and a favourite among in-the-know Westerners and visitors as well as locals. It is handily located too, around the corner from Nathan Road. You should book ahead because it is always packed.

Above from far left: Chinese waffles; invitingly chilled white wine; fresh fish; chicken's feet are an acquired taste.

Eating is the focus of many a night out in Hong Kong, but there's no shortage of other kinds of nightlife in the urban centres. A massive arts complex is planned close to the ICC and Kowloon Station in West Kowloon, but passions about what kind of dedicated venues should and shouldn't be included, and the final design, have led to the project being continually delayed. For now, many of Hong Kong's entertainment venues – particularly the larger, government-run, ones – are multi-purpose, and offer mixed programmes of dance, classical and contemporary music, theatre and film.

Theatre, Classical Music and Dance

Fringe Club

2 Lower Albert Road, Central; tel: 2521 7251; www.hkfringeclub.com; MTR: Central

Housed in a 19th-century ice house and dairy depot, the Fringe is Hong Kong's foremost centre for alternative arts, with a small theatre and studio, galleries and a rooftop garden and restaurant. The programme includes jazz, avant-garde music and rock. *See also p.28 and p.29.*

Hong Kong Academy for Performing Arts

1 Gloucester Road, Wan Chai; tel: 2584 8500; www.hkapa.edu; MTR: Wan Chai

The APA, as it is known, puts on courses in every field from television to Chinese opera. It also contains the Lyric Theatre – used by the Hong Kong repertory and visiting companies – and presents fine concerts by its own students and international musicians. It is often used as a venue during the Arts Festival. *See also p.48 and p.50.*

Hong Kong Arts Centre

2 Harbour Road, Wan Chai; tel: 2582 0200; www.hkac.org.hk; MTR: Wan Chai

As well as containing art galleries and the Agnès b cinema, this venue hosts theatre groups (some in English). *See also p.48 and p.50.*

Hong Kong City Hall

5 Edinburgh Place, Central; tel: 2921 2840; www.cityhall.gov.hk; MTR: Central/Hong Kong

City Hall contains a 1,424-seat concert hall and a theatre that hosts Chinese opera and Western music, as well as festival events.

Hong Kong Cultural Centre

10 Salisbury Road, Tsim Sha Tsui, Kowloon; tel: 2734 9011; www.hkculturalcentre.gov.hk; MTR: Tsim Sha Tsui

Located on the Kowloon waterfront is Hong Kong's premier arts venue, with three fine auditoria and many other facilities. It hosts most performances put on by the Hong Kong Philharmonic and the Hong Kong Chinese Orchestra and many visiting artists, as well as musicals. There are also frequent free concerts and activities, especially during the daytime. *See also p.63.*

Other Music Venues

AsiaWorld-Expo Arena

AsiaWorld-Expo, Hong Kong International Airport, Lantau; tel: 3608 8828; www.asiaworld-expo.com; MTR: AsiaWorld-Expo

This 13,500-seat hall has opened up Hong Kong to a flow of suitably giant-scale pop acts. Recent visitors include Green Day, Muse and DJ Seb Fontaine. It is part of the AsiaWorld-Expo site and has its own MTR station.

Grappa's Cellar

Basement Jardine House, 1 Connaught Place, Central; tel: 2521 2582; www.elgrande.com.hk; MTR: Central/Hong Kong

Family-style Italian restaurant hosts a decent range of live music gigs. Tickets usually packaged with drinks or food.

Hong Kong Convention and Exhibition Centre

1 Expo Road, Wan Chai; tel: 2582 8888; www.hkcec.com; MTR: Wan Chai

Once the trade fairs are packed up, HKCEC also hosts many visiting live acts: Oasis, Tom Jones and Roger Waters have all played here. *See also p.48 and p.51.*

Peel Fresco Music Lounge

49 Peel Street, Central; tel: 2540 2046; www.peelfresco.com; MTR: Central

Tucked away in a SoHo nook, this bohemian-style lounge bar puts on live jazz most nights. A mix of free and paid events.

Rockschool

2/F, 21–25 Luard Road, Wan Chai; tel: 2510 7339; MTR: Wan Chai

By music-lovers, for music-lovers. This roomy venue provides a stage for local bands and aspiring artists. Opens as a pub during the day, so drop in for lunch or a drink and find out what's on.

Cinema

Broadway Cinémathèque

3 Public Square Street, Yau Ma Tei; tel: 2388 0002; www.bc.cinema. com.hk; MTR: Yau Ma Tei

A mix of mainstream movies, foreign and arthouse releases, plus a film library, café *(see p.68)* and regular events. Hong Kong's first stop for cinephiles.

iSquare

7/F 63 Nathan Road, Tsim Sha Tsui; tel: 3516 8811; www.uacinemas. com.hk; MTR: Tsim Sha Tsui

The new iSquare has two standard theatres, two VIP theatres and a huge IMAX cinema with a 21m by 12m (70 by 40ft) screen.

The Palace IFC

Level 1, IFC Mall, Central; tel: 2388 6268; www.cinema.com.hk; MTR: Hong Kong

The Palace has five small cosy theatres showing current releases. Smart café, book, DVD and gift shop in the foyer.

Bars

The Backyard

Langham Place Hotel, 555 Shanghai Street, Mong Kok; tel: 3552 3250; MTR: Mong Kok

Above from far left: Fringe Club for alternative arts events; live band at Grappa's Cellar.

Mong Kok's most stylish option for drinks with an urban view. Kick back on the loungers and beanbags and enjoy cocktails by the glass or jug.

Bahama Mama's

4–5 Knutsford Terrace, Tsim Sha Tsui; tel: 2368 2121; MTR: Tsim Sha Tsui

Caribbean-inspired bar with a mix of front terrace, dance floor where you can sway to reggae and funk beats, and table football for the non-rhythmic.

Delaney's

G–1/F, One Capital Place, 18 Luard Road, Wan Chai; tel: 2804 2880; MTR: Wan Chai

A popular Irish pub, serving draught Guinness and good pub food. The giant screen upstairs shows rugby and football matches. There's another lively branch at 71–77 Peking Road, Tsim Sha Tsui (tel: 2301 3980).

Dragon-i

UG/F The Centrium, 60 Wyndham Street, Central; tel: 3110 1222; www.dragon-i.com.hk; MTR: Central

By night this restaurant and club is a celeb hang-out. Book ahead to eat and be ready to win over doormen to party.

East End Brewery

Sunning Plaza, 10 Hysan Avenue, Causeway Bay; tel: 2577 9119; MTR: Causeway Bay

Casual outdoor bar with a good selection of beers, including imported microbrews and house brews. The covered terrace, popular on warm evenings, is shared with the adjacent Inn Side Out, which serves American-style fare.

Pier 7

Viewing Deck, Central Pier 7; tel: 2167 8377; www.igors.com.hk; MTR: Hong Kong

Located on the top of the Central Star Ferry terminal, Pier 7's outdoor deck faces the major Central skyscrapers and is open to the public, so order from the bar. Lengthy wine list and wallet-friendly happy hour 6–9pm, with free nibbles.

Phoenix

29 Shelley Street, Mid-Levels; tel: 2546 2110; MTR: Central

Charming venue that gives gastro pubs a good name. Extensive selection of wine by the glass and daily blackboard menu. Two-for-one happy hour from 4pm to 8pm daily. Keep on the Mid-Levels Escalator until Mosque Street.

Staunton's

10 Staunton Street, Central; tel: 2973 6611; MTR: Central

Top spot for day-time cappuccinos and night-time people-watching, right next to the Mid-Levels Escalator and busy seven nights a week.

The Waterfront

58 Yung Shue Wan Main Street, Lamma; tel: 2982 1168

Five minutes from the ferry pier, just off Lamma's main street, The Waterfront offers substantial global fare, but it's the view and location you come for. One of the best places to take in the sunset.

CREDITS

Insight Step by Step Hong Kong
Written by: Ruth Williams, Joseph R. Yogerst
Updated by: Ruth Williams
Series Editor: Clare Peel
Cartography Editor: James Macdonald
Picture Managers: Steve Lawrence
Photography by: Apa/Alex Havret, except:
Apa/Glyn Genin 88T, 89B, 90B/T; Apa/Sinopix
8–9, 14 margin top, 15TL, 17BR, 61TR, 78T, 80B,
83TL, 86B, 89T; Apa/Taras Kovaliv 26 margin
top; Alamy 59B, 74B, 83B, 84, 87T, 92, 108, 115;
Axiom 79B; Caseneac 124; Corbis 11TR, 23T,
54B, 75, 77B, 78B, 91T; Eyevine 51T; FRCMike
122; Getty 63; Courtesy of Harbour View Inter-
national House 109; Courtesy of Hong Kong
Tourist Board 21T, 26B, 42T, 42C, 43B, 50, 53T,
55, 56TL, 58B, 64TL, 65TR, 67B, 69B, 70B, 79T;
Courtesy of Island Shangri-La 111; Kobal 53B;
Tom le Bas 92B; Manfred Morgenstern 22; On
Asia 85; David Vidier 123; Dave Wilkinson 76T,
77T; World Picture News 74T. **Cover**: main
image: Getty; front left: istock photo; front right:
Apa/Alex Havret.
Printed by: CTPS-China.

Second Edition 2010

www.insightguides.com

DISTRIBUTION

Worldwide
APA Publications GmbH & Co. Verlag KG
(Singapore branch)
7030 Ang Mo Kio Ave 5, 08-65 Northstar @ AMK
Singapore 569880
Tel: (65) 570 1051
E-mail: apasin@singnet.com.sg

UK and Ireland
GeoCenter International Ltd
Meridian House, Churchill Way West
Basingstoke, Hampshire, RG21 6YR
Tel: (44) 01256 817 987
E-mail: sales@geocenter.co.uk

United States
Langenscheidt Publishers, Inc.
36–36 33rd Street, 4th Floor
Long Island City, NY 11106
Tel: (1) 718 784 0055
E-mail: orders@langenscheidt.com

Australia
Universal Publishers
1 Waterloo Road, Macquarie Park, NSW 2113
Tel: (61) 2 9857 3700
E-mail: sales@universalpublishers.com.au

New Zealand
Hema Maps New Zealand Ltd (HNZ)
Unit 2, 10 Cryers Road
East Tamaki, Auckland 2013
Tel: (64) 9 273 6459
E-mail: sales.hema@clear.net.nz

CONTACTING THE EDITORS

We would appreciate it if readers would alert us
to errors or outdated information by writing to
us at insight@apaguide.co.uk or Apa Publications,
PO Box 7910, London SE1 1WE, UK.

INDEX

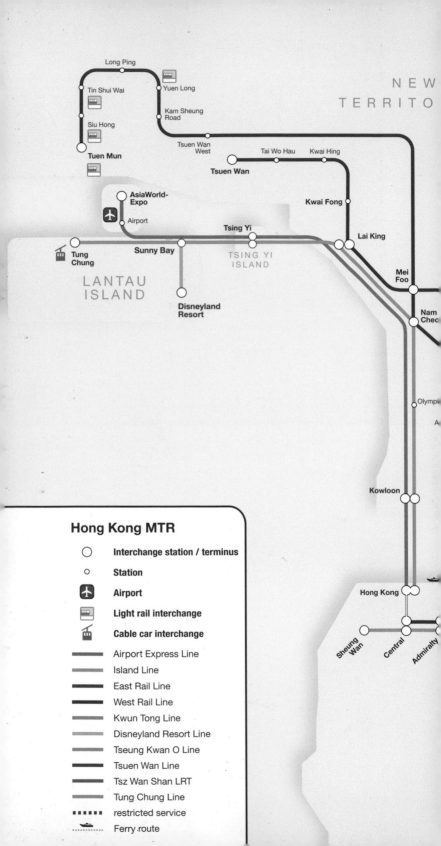